The Cat's Reincarnation: Transformative Encounters with Animals

Dr. Laurie Alison Moore with Jessie Justin Joy

www.animiracles.com

lauriemoore.sessions.seminars@Gmail.com

831-477-7007

Copyright 2013

by Dr. Laurie Moore

No part of this book may be used or reproduced without the permission of Laurie A. Moore:

lauriemoore.sessions.seminars@Gmail.com

831-477-7007 Laurie@DrLaurieMoore.com

Forward by Dean Bernal

Cover by Mike de Give:

www.graphicsmonterey.com

Editor: Kathy Glass

Photography: Ray Torres

ISBN-10 1484956206

ISBN 13 is 9781484956205

Acknowledgments

Thank you to my love, kind and sweet Ray, for being a pure channel of gratitude, peace, love, and unconditional support. Thank you to my beloved feline guru, son, and friend Jessie Justin Joy, for being a beacon of joy, peace, light, and love.

Foreword by Dean Bernal

Shocking yet true, during particular historical eras, some societies have mistakenly thought that women were less valuable than men, people of color were less valuable than people of white skin, and children were less valuable than adults. Many societies still believe that animals are less worthy of honor and respect than humans. Many people continue to think that animals are less intelligent than humans. An animal's wisdom is often overlooked when we do not comprehend their language or culture

Dr. Laurie Moore's book shines light on valuable wisdom that animals intend to impart to humans. She offers the perspective that animal culture is richly loving in consciously astute ways. Dr. Laurie Moore's book is very personal, able to touch each of our hearts. She includes herself as an ongoing learner in the process of her storytelling.

Dr Laurie trusts what she sees, feels, and hears yet does not impose this on anyone as a dogma. She relays how her heart is touched by birds, felines, canines, whales, dolphins, moths, lizards, trees, flowers, and other beings who share the planet with us. She believes that animals are superb permaculturists, far ahead of humans.

Her powerful experience with Jessie Justin Joy, a soul-mate cat who reincarnates, is a life-turning point for Dr. Laurie. Jessie takes Laurie on a journey into timelessness and space-awareness void of physical separateness. Here she finds that one eternity exists, holding all other fleeting realities of feeling, thought, and occurrence.

Dr. Laurie's love for her cat companion allows her to open a door, back into the state of childhood innocence. From this place she can hear, see, and feel the elements of a world that is unconditional and constant in warm awakening. This is the world that the animals know as life. By entering this paradigm, she can converse effortlessly with animals and insects of any species.

Readers have the opportunity to discover their own personal journeys through the experiences that Dr. Laurie shares. She gently prods us to find our own ability to hear, feel, and see the communications of animals.

Like people, every individual animal has a unique personality. When given the opportunity, an animal will share his or her perceptions. Dr. Laurie listens deeply to the hearts of animals, respecting their voices. She wrote this book as a messenger of particular animal teachers.

While the book is born in the realm of awakened consciousness, Dr. Laurie takes all lessons she learns as maps for the practical and emotional human world. Using her extensive background as a therapist, combined with her many years of study on spiritual paths, she offers us a way of living that expresses the reality of unconditional love.

Dr. Laurie shares her stories with you as incentive. She believes that each human can find his or her most important dream of heart inside themselves and in the world to which they artistically add their uniqueness. What she brings to our lives is the necessary nourishment for that seed of evolutionary benevolence alive in each soul. That small seed has the potential to bloom into a flower that turns each individual's world into a magical journey of unconditional love.

      Dr. Laurie credits the animals as being co-writers of this book, especially Jessie Justin Joy, her feline friend and teacher, so enjoy your journey with them.

Dean Bernal, Executive Director
JoJo Dolphin Project www.marinewildlife.org
Dolphin, Whale, and Marine Wildlife Foundation
Please Note:
Occasionally names, identifying details, or sequences in this book have been changed to protect privacy or emphasize the messages brought forth.

Introduction

It is the summer of 2004, and I choose an outdoor meditation-sanctuary spot. My intention is to deeply connect with animals while I sit in silence each day. Many animals come to merge with and guide me. In the beginning, many come through the inner spirit realms without appearing in the physical realm. When my heart is trusting and open, they show up. As time goes on, I desire physical proof that the animals are truly reaching out. I request to know if I experience their messages rather than my projections. Soon a green frog decides to meditate with me in my sacred place.

On a walk near our home with Ray, my mate, a little lizard approaches us. I tell her with all my heart, "I love you." She darts to me, scurries up my back, and joins us for the walk. My trust in the Divine is magnified profoundly by this experience. This sweet lizard comes to connect and teach. She answers my question, affirming my trust in the communications I had been receiving.

Neighborhood dogs begin to visit, sometimes showing up right on time to attend seminars that I teach, leaving at the end along with the others. A bobcat makes daily visits. Coyotes share their lives with me. Hawks, ravens, and hummingbirds become my friends.

One afternoon in my meditation spot, I feel as though my cells have begun to expand. Soon I discover that life is very fluid.* Golden light changes my experience of my body. I find that endless life flows playfully through consciousness in my heart. I recognize this assistance to be the joyous dolphins opening me up to new worlds. They bring great delight and laughter to me often. They bring me sacred, playful, and fun-filled joy beyond the emotional delight I once knew as "happiness." They take me to a state of dancing ecstasy, inviting me into the celebration of existence. Sheer glee is permitted within the fabric of any mood and thought. I have yet to meet these family members in person. Soon doors open up quite unexpectedly. I find myself traveling to Hawaii often, accompanied by groups who wish to swim and communicate with our cetacean friends.

My cat-beloved, Jessie Justin Joy, helps me connect to all the animals with his love and ability to gently guide me from within. I consider the animals to be my role models of the highest type of existence. JJJ and others have taught me unconditional kindness, unconditional joy, and unconditional love. They have shown me that the way to be kind, happy, and loving is to enter the forever-opening realms of these qualities, which go beyond assumptions of how any situation might develop. These qualities are of the heart, here for everyone. These qualities are the answers to mysterious and penetrating heart-yearning.

Time and time again, I find that clear intentions about one's imagined manifestations lead to imperfect yet cherished results. Focusing on what is not desired tends to lead to encountering more of it. People have been able to comprehend and implement these truths. I do. Then I forget. Then I do better. Then I forget. Then I fine-tune details. I notice that my cat Jessie treats everyone with compassion regardless of their remembering or forgetting.

I notice that animals are masters of living by intention. Animals do not complicate life with intricate thoughts and mental exercises. They tend to operate from their heart. Their directions come from their heart-born purposes. After many years of focusing on people, I decide that I have much to learn from animals and nature.

Each evening during my quest I soak in the bathtub, filling myself with the scents of rose, geranium, vanilla, sandalwood, and amber. These simple scents give me great nourishment, and the water gives me great comfort. The whale visits me while I am in the bathtub after Gina Palmer, an animal communicator, suggests that I listen to the whale. The whale ushers me into a state of all-peaceful oneness beyond words.

Several months later I am in Molokai, Hawaii, where again my minds begins to doubt the experience. Was that really the whale who made contact? I call out to sea, "Please show me it is you that I am hearing, great whale." Canine Charcoal Beauty repeatedly comes to me when I am willing to enter the heaven realms within the creation of my heart. He leaves me to myself when I exit those realms. Now he is by my side. I sit and he stands on a rock as we look yonder. Within a minute I see something huge shoot out of the water and come down with a big splash. A moment later the biggest tail I have ever seen waves for many minutes from at least a mile away. The whale has come.

The magical trip continues. When I share my experiences on Dolphinville.com radio, I feel the cetaceans moving their big expanded joy through me. The night before the radio webcast, beings emerge from the ocean who cover me with a robe of light-crystals, informing me that I may wear this garment to feel safe from interfering energies. When I put my messages out into the world, I wear this robe. Life feels more and more like a magical fairy tale. Trust in vast realms of magic deepens within my belly.

The cetaceans offer unlimited openness and welcome. "Come into the arms of the Divine. Come home and we shall help you. We are your friends." They greet and invite many into big-bellied joyous laughter, playful splashes, and breaths of love. The dolphins help me to enjoy the duality realities as adventurous fun. They remind me to accept my human-hood with great aliveness and joy!

The whale is living in oneness. When I slide back into duality awareness I lose the connection. To find the whale I return to oneness. The whale brings me to only One. One love. One peace. One life in all beings, all faces, all enactments. How I love the dolphins! I try to say I love the whale and I do ... but she slips out of my consciousness when I love her because she is oneness. I am her. She is me. There was no me loving her or her loving me--in the whale reality, there is only love in motion. We are.

Many months later, back in California, I am frustrated with my own species: human being. I grow tired of hearing problems in the office. I begin to feel dried out. I feel like everything I have to give has been taken. I look at myself in the mirror. My eyes look youthful but I feel suddenly very old—wrinkled inside. I drink glass after glass of water. I smear lotion on my body again and again, but deep within I feel wrung out to the core. I have become a washcloth that is stiff and hard. I get into the bathtub. Inside myself, I feel the water is missing. I go outside, where I call to the cetaceans from my meditation spot. Soon everything around me appears fluid, but deep inside I am not part of the fluidity.

    I drink water, saying, "I love you, water" and "Thank you water." I offer dolphins and whales the love pouring through my heart in circles and colors of water. It is as though they live inside me and simultaneously, I live inside of their hearts. The miles become meaningless.

    Space and time lose form. I am made of abundant fresh streaming water. I feel myself to be shared and received as the nourishing water. Feeling the dolphins satiated, I become full. Together we ripple warmly into the air extending far beyond our bodies.

    The dolphins and whales continue to give back to me until I overflow. However, this is experienced as all life giving to itself while dolphins, whales, and I are part of this one occurrence. I become a stream within. The water fills me. I am made of water. I am fluid. I am cool as the river with the depth of her running through me. I pray for a direct line to the Divine. A moment later I decide that all my concerns about anything are meaningless. I donate the energy that the judgments, comparisons, pet peeves, and gripes were made of to the sun, who takes all that fuel, turning it back to the one love. The sun warms the water running through me.

    I have been loved by water and here my story begins.

    Note: These are natural states available to humanity, invoked by the Divine Mother with the animals as ushers. The states of which I speak were not invoked with any type of drugs. These paradigms of reality are available to the open-hearted, opened-souled. Ask to be taken into these realms with the animals, and you may remember that these realms are a part of you. Those who meditate often find easier access but not every requires formal meditation to arrive in these sates of awareness.

The Cat's Reincarnation and Unconditional Trust in Love

Blessed Thrice I Find Contentment

I decide to live with a cat so I drive straight to the SPCA (Society for the Prevention of Cruelty to Animals). I plan to find a feminine kitten. Among the felines is a huge boy with the biggest smiling cheeks I have ever seen on a cat. He says "meow" to me in a very deep chirping voice. Tiger-striped and big as a bobcat he is. I fall in love.

The next day I am back to pick him up. Each feline has been switched to a different cubby. The room is cluttered with barks and meows that do not harmonize. I can't find him. I sigh. It isn't meant to be. Immediately I hear a chirping meow in that unique deep male tone. I look behind me. My tiger man is looking right at me. I bring him home.

Wednesday, day a neighbor named Kristine stops by. When Kristine enters, Jessie disappears. Kristine and I look everywhere. No tiger man under the bed. No feline in the closet.

I had believed that cats need to stay inside for several days when moving to a new abode. They need to scent their territory so that they can return to their dwelling. Cats are masters with olfactory senses. How is he going to get back after only a day in his new home? I keep the car door and the apartment windows open. I sit in my apartment where late night is filling the room, the white cotton curtains kept open. I fall into the hours as they pass, beginning to immerse myself in my own misery.

I answer the ringing phone with great hope that he's been found. It's Kristine. "He's not back yet," I say.

The phone rings again. It's my dad. I clutch the phone to try to keep my voice from trembling out in broken tones. I feel sliced in two. I have already fallen so deeply in love with my Jessie-Boy that my heart aches as though I have lost a family member of decades. Each minute the clock number turns loudly. The door remains an open invitation. It gets quieter and colder. My thoughts get faster and louder. Is he gone?

"What's the matter?" asks Dad. The apartment is partially fresh with the nearby ocean ions. Simultaneously the air is tangled with despair. My heart is crumpled into a ball. I look at the wicker waste basket. Picking up a piece of paper from the floor I aim. Basket. Despair hits. I toss my tears, "My cat is lost."

"Meow!" It is my boy with his deep male voice, knowing gaze, and black and gray furry tiger stripes. He is looking up at me and reassuring me that he is back home and that he loves me.

Ruby, a friend from college, moves in next door. This town is a magnet that has become home, grabbing her back with centrifugal force, You reunite with familiar scents, nature scenery, and personalities. Hence, eight years later Laurie with graduate degree and budding career meets Ruby with fiancé and budding hopes in front of Nature's Health Foods, which is about to close. The time: twelve noon. The reason: synchronistic magnetism. Ruby's great hopes and Laurie's great hopes have come to work as one. We meet to help each other. We will turn some of our dreams into rainwater and feel rich. We will share a garden, watching vegetable leaves catch glittering raindrops in their palms. We will feast on life's promises.

Some days we will leave the windows open by mistake. Water vapor will cover the inside of our apartments. Like the children we were, unnoticing yet alert, we will be drenched in joy. Unfortunately, joy that is attached to certain expectations soon becomes mold, and a lot of clean-up work is in store. Somewhere deep in the human consciousness this is known, but at thirty years of age it can be blocked out so as to start the adventure fresh and innocent, trusting that all will be easy.

Every evening at sundown, Ruby goes on a walk with her cat, Kitten-Charm. Often Jessie is invited. I arrive home Tuesday evening. Jessie doesn't greet me at the car to walk me in as he usually does. I roll down my window. Without his meow to fill up my ears, I notice that traffic sounds like an argument. Nobody stands by my feet when I get out of my car. I am immediately worried.

Ruby knocks firmly. A stench has arisen in my home. An apple is rotting in the fruit bowl so I scoop it up into a paper towel. The air is laced with uncertainty. Walking outdoors toward the compost bucket, we talk. I chuck the apple and ask her about her day while scanning the yard for Jessie. When we get back inside I notice that her red hair goes well with the royal-blue pillows

A stench has arisen in my home. An apple is rotting in the fruit bowl so I scoop it up into a paper towel. The air is laced with uncertainty. Walking outdoors toward the compost bucket, we talk. I chuck the apple and ask her about her day while scanning the yard for Jessie. When we get back inside I notice that her red hair goes well with the royal-blue pillows. Life's scenery seems to fit well into life itself at all times. I wonder why she is visiting so late. Maybe she's having problems with her fiancé and needs to talk.

"Are you alright?" I ask while I look out the window, scanning for Jessie.

She explains that Jessie disappeared while they were on a walk. She suggests we go back to the spot of his disappearance.

We head out past the apartment complex

Passing by a hanging wisteria vine and inhaling sweetness, we look for my boy. Ruby says, "This is where he disappeared."

"Jessie!" I call.

"MEOW!"

The three of us run home with Jessie in the lead. I am thrice blessed. Lost and found again, Jessie will always stay with me, I feel.

More Than Enough Love to Go Around

"Have you seen a cat named Jessie?" an unfamiliar woman asks from underneath her huge pink beach hat. She is hovering over my lawn chair. Her question startles me more than her sudden presence. I am enjoying the sun as it soaks into my heart.

"Jessie, the cat?"

"Yes, he's a good friend. I come to visit him every day." Her response drifts above me for a minute, mingling subtly with the scent of freshly cut grass. Did I hear her right?

"The cat?"

"Yes. I visit him every day."

"Right here," I point. He's under my lawn chair, purring. That's my boy. Cats, squirrels, and people visit Jessie frequently. One morning I even find a woman looking through my living room window for him.

"Can I help you?" I ask.

"I'm looking for Jessie."

"You must be Jessie's person," says another new neighbor. "I'm Samantha. He came to welcome me and introduce himself the first day I moved in."

"Hi Laurie," says Michelle from two doors down. "Have you seen Jessie? It's time for his midday treat."

"What kind of treat?" My cat has diabetes so I need to be careful.

"Two protein snack biscuits for cats. He gets them every day at one. Is that alright?"

"That's wonderful. Thanks, Michelle."

"Treat time, Jessie!"

Jessie stays put, purring under my lawn chair.

"That's funny," Michelle says. "When you're not home he runs on over as soon as I call. He comes inside." With his many friends and companions, Jessie consistently manages to be home when I am.

After the two of us are on very familiar terms, Jessie is hungry one evening while I am with a client. Jessie jumps on my lap, looks me in the eyes fondly, and says "Meow."

This means 'I'm ready for dinner.' Since I am not going to interrupt the session I pet him, continuing to listen to the new client, who is describing her concerns in detail.

Jessie jumps up on the back of the chair, swooshing his tail in front of my face repeatedly. I chuckle while my client looks serious. At last Jessie heads into the kitchen, where he loudly taps his bowl on the ground. My client and I are both laughing together now.

On Jessie's first night home he got into bed with me, faced me, bit the tip of my nose gently for a kiss, curled up and turned a little circle, smushed his back against my chest, and went to sleep. This routine continued each night. One night he takes to sleeping outside in a chair. What have I done?

Ruby tells me about a cat communicator named Gina Palmer. I have not yet recognized my own gift. I hear, see, and feel animal messages regularly but do not yet trust this. Gina speaks with a voice that rests in her heart.

She tells me that Jessie loves me very much and that we aligned as similar souls with matching purposes. However, he has recently brought me a wedding ring in the form of a captured bird. His intention was to cement the relationship, letting me know that he will be staying with me permanently.

Gina is right about the bird. I had not comprehended his intention before. I had called a rescue agency to help me save the bird while keeping Jessie temporarily out of the bathroom, where I attempted to help the bird. The message Jessie communicated to Gina went something like this: "Laurie not interested in my life outside the apartment. She doesn't appreciate my hunting skills or come outside with me to learn about my world."

Feeling rejected, Jessie had taken to sleeping on the chair outside, right after the gift was misunderstood. Trust toward Gina begins to grow. A few days after my session with Gina, Jessie presents a squirrel. I thank him, congratulate him on his expert hunting skills, and get on the phone to tell some friends about the wonderful gift, letting the dead squirrel stay in the living room for a while. After an hour I take the squirrel out for a burial while Jessie is outside. I say a blessing for the squirrel wonderful gift, letting the dead squirrel stay in the living room for a while. After an hour I take the squirrel out for a burial while Jessie is outside. I say a blessing for the squirrel soul, clearly no longer in that body. Upon his return, Jessie runs to the spot where the squirrel has been, next running to me to sniff my mouth. He checks to see if I ate the generous present. My feline pal and I are best friends again. I receive my nightly nose kiss and dream-time cuddling.

Living with Two Guys
My mate says with a voice that is thick and tasty like maple syrup, "Come near to get as close to my heart as you can."

I believe he means me but Jessie jumps on the bed, mushing himself against our heads. The sprinkler system comes on. The window is near the garden so I hear it. Ruby is outside watering, completely enjoying her delicious fantasy of what is to come next. I can sense it. Ruby and I articulate beautiful fantasies to one another and then we make them come true. Ruby has been very inspired by watching me delight in my dream boyfriend after years of struggle with someone else. When I was suffering, her pendulum and flowers seeping through the thin apartment wall kept me dreaming up a joyful future. Now that my joyful future is here, she's drinking it in for inspiration.

I snuggle closer to my precious Ray. "Jessie," I say, "Ray and I need privacy when we make love." Jessie stays right where he is but politely turns around and faces the other direction, looking out the window and viewing the creek outside. Water, playfully running over stones by our window, chimes joy in the air. Now, whenever I kiss my guy, Jessie quickly turns around to face away. He makes us laugh.

I call Gina again because Jessie takes to pouncing on my face every morning at 9 a.m.

"Tell Laurie I wish to spend more time with her at home instead of going to the vet so much. She's too busy with unimportant things and she's oversleeping because she's not happy being busy. Rush, rush, rush. Get up and enjoy the day, Laurie!" I laugh loudly.

Jessie Teaches Me the Nature of Pure Joy

Early July
One day I wake up to children's voices bouncing along with their bodies on a trampoline in the courtyard. I like my life but there is consistent fear in my heart. I am constantly scared that Jessie's illnesses will take him away.

A week after my friend moved in, the vet informed me that he had hepatitis, diabetes, a broken pelvis, parasites, a sore throat, a missing toe on an unhealed foot, and the need to have half his colon removed in order to live. He now visits a
holistic vet, a chiropractor, and an energy healer.

I worry that Jessie may not be here as long as I need him. I need him to stay forever. The green carpet is soft under my feet. My hands feel smooth while I rub them with watermelon cream. I worry that I will never feel secure. The house is full of summer and cinnamon. This is the night that my boy disappears.

That Evening
My fingers are clutching the phone so hard that I dig half moons into my palms with my

fingernails, only half realizing. My throat is shrinking thin as a straw. My stomach feels full of thunder and lightning. I am shaking. I am calling Gina Palmer after work hours, praying that she answers the phone. "Gina, my boy did not come home at night like he always does. Please locate him."

Two Days Later
Jessie's body has been attacked and silenced by coyotes. He may not make it. First, he assures me via Gina that he is still on the planet but stranded in a tree. According to Gina, Jessie went off with a tortoise-shell and homeless neighborhood cat
who taught him a game of teasing wild dogs. I assume this means coyotes. Jessie and the other cat got in a tree to tease the coyotes but now my boy is in trouble. He's been stranded there for twelve hours. The coyotes, still below, are mad. He
tells Gina to let me know that he is very sorry to worry me. It was not his plan.

    This sounds like my boy. I have observed him to chase huge dogs, have a nonchalant attitude around raccoons, and hang out around deer. I once saw a deer kiss Jessie on the nose. When I email Gina six hours later—after searching every tree in the neighborhood and by the creek—Jessie has gone blank. Gina, who has known him for three years, cannot locate him.

"I think I may have used up my ninth life," he laughs and says to Annette Betcher, another animal communicator who is an expert at locating missing animals.

"Jessie's body has been dragged. He played dead and tried to get back to you. But he's up to his last breaths. Don't worry. This cat wants to get back to you. He will be back within a month or so. Some cats do come back in a new body. He's very sure about that."

The adventures of living with my sweet feline friend flash before me. I think of our cuddling, our outdoor time, and his mentoring of a little kitten named Buster. Buster followed Jessie everywhere, copying Jessie's every move. Together they spent mornings chatting, playing, meditating.

I remember asking the SPCA to make certain I was taking home a healthy cat. When it turned out that my new friend had many health challenges I was very happy they had not known. Jessie was indeed the one and only cat for me.

But the universe had other plans in store for me than what I imagined. Avoiding loss was not an option. Finding eternity was. When Jessie and I first got home from the SPCA, which was a five-minute drive from my apartment, I knew I would stay with Jessie forever. The mysterious Source knew that Jessie was going to assist in teaching me that the pain of separation is an inner state rather than an outer one.

I check my emails. Gina has a message for me. "Jessie says his abandonment issues are healed, thanks to your relationship. He is feeling completely fulfilled and at peace emotionally because of you. His body problems are due to lack of care before he met you. He wants you to know this and not to blame yourself. He says these conditions are the result of his own karmic journey and not a reflection on your care."

I fed Jessie through a tube four times a day when he needed it, and he got strong again. I nursed him back after his bout with cat anemia and anorexia—the result of having half his colon removed because of the broken pelvis that had healed inadequately due to a lack of medical care before moving in with me. Any time I slept away from home, I drove back at six in the morning, cutting plans short to give him his insulin twice a day. Whatever Jessie needed, he had. Debt meant nothing. Jessie came first. He was estimated to be four when we met. Apparently no medical care was provided to him until his week at the SPCA and then after moving in with me. That was partly why he was a giant. He wasn't neutered until he stayed at the SPCA hotel, so his hormones had allowed him to get very big. He was from the streets and fearless. I loved him immediately.

    Once when he had an insulin attack I rushed him to the animal hospital. He was so limp in my arms I thought he was almost dead, but I looked into his loving eyes and said, "Jessie, hang on. We're almost there." Ray was driving. "Hold on. I love you, and you will be okay. Just hold on a few more minutes."

    A few hours later Jessie was home with his head upside down on the ground and his back slumped over. I ran outside assuming he had fainted, but my boy was happily looking down a gopher hole, delighted with life, delighted with himself, and delighted with us!

Jessie's excitement with life sparks my yearning. What can I do to have as much fun as he does searching in the ground? I haven't bowled for fifteen years. Maybe I'll call a group of friends to get together and go bowling. Maybe a trip to Hawaii. A day at the beach always tastes exciting. Maybe I'll sign up for a community television class. Something inside me, much more fulfilling and joyful than my outward searching, pulls. Some unnamable enthusiasm, the ripe thoughts of observance, touch the place that is yearning. I breathe the evening air. I am in awe. I am fulfilled being right here.

"He's come back home to you with another body," Annette assures me now. "He says he will be back very soon."

It dawns upon me that I had been praying for my boy's body to be fully healthy, and after those six thousand dollars' worth of Western operations, Eastern remedies, herbs, trials with special diets, and daily insulin shots, he was much better off but still suffering physically. If Annette is right, perhaps my dream for my boy's health is going to come true in an unexpected way. Perhaps my prayer is being answered.

As soon as Annette hangs up I lose the enthusiasm. I find myself shuffling that momentary hope back into the deck, and picking out a card of sorrow. In my house I feel Jessie everywhere but he's not home. I try to be happy for his spiritual presence, but I am in a state of profound despair and distrust with Spirit. Jessie's body being missing has left me weeping from my belly.

I'm crying, and then laughing. Simultaneously a new kind of wonder is growing inside me. I feel like there is a garden in my heart. I feel Jessie right inside me. Something new is being nurtured here. At the same time, my usual habits of thought and worry are speaking frequently in my mind. Something else is calling me. I can't quite pinpoint it, but it feels like I am being nourished and spoken to deep within. In moments between the adrenaline, I feel an unfamiliar peace and questioning of everything with new openness.

Five Weeks Later

Jessie, via Gina, informs me that he can enter a new cat body
if I pick one out. Too much for me to believe. Annette however agrees with Gina. A psychic attends a class I am teaching unexpectedly, saying she has a message from my cat. "He is coming back and wants me to tell you." Three messengers agree. I open up to the idea.

Ray says he doesn't know when I ask him if he thinks it is true. With eyes that soften my muscles and soothe my jumping ideas, he calms me. He's open. He doesn't take a rigid position or stance of certainty in either direction. I feel more settled. His skin is dark and very smooth. He has Spanish and Jewish ancestors, and he was raised in laid-back New Orleans. He moved to California at twenty-two to study yoga. He smiles with very circular bright eyes like a young boy.

I receive a voice mail: "My name is Stacey Caldwell. I live at the end of your street. I don't have your cat and I'm sorry you lost him. I received your missing cat notice in my mailbox. I have five kittens that are all five weeks old. Would you like one?"

"No" slams down in my mind. Nobody but Jessie, and then it dawns on me. He is coming back and he's trying to get through. He reincarnated in a neighbor's house to make it easy to find me. He had her call me. So when I return her call and she confirms that two of the kittens are tiger-striped, I am sure I am on the right track! I'm back in a fairy tale. The Divine is working in a fun way!

I'm the kind of person that ends up with a cat in my lap wherever I go. They love me. They think I'm one of them. How will I explain this reincarnation business to the woman? Probably won't. I'll just tell her that cats like me. When Jessie runs straight to me she will be surprised and delighted that her kitten found his new mother. If I mention the reincarnation she may think I'm crazy. Or maybe she will just feel sorry for me and assume that I'm making this up to avoid the grief. Or maybe she will believe me. But most important of all, she will know which cat is for me because Jessie will run to me immediately.

I arrive and the cats ignore me.

"They haven't met a lot of people yet, so they are shy." Stacey seems embarrassed. I am. I approach the kittens and they run to all four corners of the living room.

"Thanks. I guess it's just not meant to be. My last cat and I had an immediate bond so I don't think I'm a good match with any of these cats. I'm looking for one who feels drawn to me. I'm not connecting really well with these cats, but thank you. It was thoughtful of you to call after getting my note." I walk home, bending a little more with each step until I arrive outside my front door and just freeze, slumped forward, staring at my old shoelaces. The door opens and Ray comes out.

"They're just not the right cats for you," Ray says reassuringly. He puts his arm around me. He smells like the garden. His shirt is soft flannel. "Come here." He squeezes me to him. "It's going to work out. More time. Life takes time." A flock of round-tummied quail dash across the street together, clicking right outside the window.

Ray's got a good outlook and it rubs off. It was the wrong phone call. Someone thought they could help and meant well, but it wasn't Jessie. That's all. He will be back. Error judgment. I'll listen to my inner feelings more closely. Intuition sends me back to the place I first met Jessie, and I wake up very excited the next day. "I'll be back in two hours." I kiss Ray, who is still dreaming.

I'm there at the SPCA when the morning is young and the place opens up. So are five other people. Today's got to be the day. Four of us want a cat. One of us has five cats to give away. I can almost feel resolution in my bones. A posted sign indicates that the SPCA is no longer open on Mondays. Well, then it must be Divine intervention. I suggest that all of us follow the man of five cats to his home and each pick one out. He agrees to it.

As I drive over nothing feels right. I'm tired. I miss the turn. I haven't eaten or even had some water. My stomach gurgles. My inspiration feels false. "Why can't this be the day?" I scream inside. Please just bring me to Jessie!

We get to the man's house, where the mother and her kittens have all disappeared. The man is perplexed. "They've never left before." Food, calls, and patience change nothing. He takes down all our names and numbers and promises to call us when they return, but he never calls. I am frustrated.

Later, as dusk drops down to my heart, as I hold my hands out to life for help, as I wish to grab the sun before it's gone, I vaguely feel what's going on within, deeper than my emotions. With my next breath, curiosity about this life adventure fills me. I am no longer lost in thoughts of desperation because I have been lit like a campfire and am made of intrigue. If I could slip into some unknown reality where cats go after life, I would find you and carry you home, dear Jessie Boy. But how do I get there? Where's the rocket to take me?

"I admire your perseverance, Sweetheart," Ray says. "Let's go looking by the creek again tomorrow and put more signs up."

It is the delicious quality in my boyfriend's voice that lets me sleep in peace. The next morning I follow a lead on a psychic who can supposedly tell me exactly where anyone or thing is located. His voice is stern. He tells me to go twenty feet northwest and three steps south. "The cat will be right there."

We use the compass. His directions lead me to a trash bin. It's empty inside and vacant outside.

I dial Gina to inform her that not only has the cat not returned, but all felines now go to great lengths to avoid me. I'm starting to get angry and am thinking twice about all this reincarnation business. Plus, my destiny has recently amounted to an empty trash bin. I think it's time I just let go.

Gina says that Jessie has a message for me.

"My Beloved Mother, Friend, Companion, Student, Laurie:

I swim in the sea of light fully awakened. I sit simultaneously here at your side. The constraints of time's bondage and conditions of body no longer are present. I am.

I am with Mother. I am with self. I am with you. We are all together as one heart. In the memory of your mind you paint me "Tiger One," while in the seat of our one heart we are the one. I sit with you through your loss of the one you hold in your memory. All the while I rest gently present inside the one heart.

Rest the questions in your mind, for I am no longer in form. I am the form of one heart. You are waiting for the event that is. I am here now with you.

You are only waiting from the place in your mind, for in the place in our heart I live! You see me in your mind's eye, and in your dream time, stretched out being with you, waving to you with my one leg, because that comforts you. Please do not follow that extension of illusion. For there you will always need to wait for me. I ask you to be present with us now.

In this precious moment beyond contemplation, beyond time, beyond mind, I am here now with you in eternity forever.

If anyone is waiting, it is me. Waiting for you to join me beyond the boundaries of mind and time, here where no one is waiting for anyone. You never release me! You release the illusion of pain and suffering by your sweet thoughts of me. For that I am grateful. For your willingness, for your presence, I give thanks. We are one another's gift.

Think of me with joy in your heart, only from a joy-filled longing. It is that longing marked with joy that attracts our reunion. That is the energy that restores
and constructs wholeness. Wholeness is the state of being that we all long to possess. While in this time of reflection, it is important that you continue your
release—your release of anything other than your joy.

Think only of the word "joy," for that energy restores the one contained within the word you call your "boy." Only this can reunite us through the longing of which you attempt to make sense.

Now is the time for you to self-nurture. Self-nurturing is your next step. Take much of the energy you once poured into me, and sometimes do pour also into your work, and pour it into yourself. Allow Ray and your clients to pour their energy into you. Your time of giving is calling for balance to your receiving. I reside now within the timeless eternity—the place where all things are formed—and I'm viewing form manifesting all at once from within the matrix of life on Earth.

I am near. I am washed into wholeness. All is well. All is complete. I live beyond time. I live without substantial form. I ask you to remove your thoughts of form and allow yourself to simply be with me. Be with mom. Be with yourself. Can you feel any comfort being here? Your challenge now is to find yourself resting within this comfort. You can do that being with me here. It is your choice.

I rest here all the while that you perform your choosing. You ask me to make choices—"to come back"? I ask you to make the only choice I have—to be here now! My circumstances of choice died with the form I laid down there with the dogs. Now I only have the quality of attraction. I am instructing you how to create the attraction that will draw me to you. You can do this from your mind. Remember, the mind creates distortions. I prefer for you to do this from your heart.

A still and quiet joy-filled heart creates a healthy body, healthy relationships. From the place within the stillness of your heart, where grief has rested, and where joy has been given birth—that is where the co-creation of me, your boy, resides.

You feel me burning bright. You see me now for who/what I am becoming. I have no more work. My work is complete while I reside here in this place. You are being asked to do your work. Your work is to become comfortable and joy-filled with receiving. You will receive me in this way."

I call Annette, who explains that Jessie says he needs to reincarnate in a big male body—no kittens! I find a beautiful smoky black cat named Shadow at the SPCA. Shadow has been living there for five weeks, having arrived the day after Jessie left our home. He's the number-one favorite of the staff, who can't figure out why nobody swooped him up immediately. This is reminiscent of Jessie's life at the SPCA when we first met, when he first gave me the big meow! He arrived. The staff favored him as one of the most loving beings there. They were shocked that he waited many weeks to go, but I was grateful that he waited until I found him!

"He doesn't need to be tiger-striped. Just make sure he's a big male and that you have an affinity for him," Annette tells me. She adds that Jessie wishes for me to understand this. However, I spend some time with Shadow and he is not Jessie at all! Not Jessie's vibe. Not Jessie's soul. Not his eyes. Nevertheless, when I call Gina and Annette they confirm that Jessie will be switching bodies with Shadow once I bring him home. This seems unfathomable to me. If I keep pushing this adventure it just might become another tragedy.

Unexpectedly, a deep rumbling laughter runs through me like a roller-coaster car full of joyous passengers. The person my feelings are becoming and the person my mind keeps thinking I am have detached from each other. I no longer understand who I am. Creation is at play inside this shifting being.

"Should I ask Shadow if it's okay with him to give up his current body?" I ask Annette.

"Absolutely not" is the response that Jessie gives to her. "Let me handle it."

"He seems convinced that you and I will get in the way. The felines must make the agreement themselves," she explains.

Friday afternoon, one hour before closing, I head to the SPCA to pick up a cat named Shadow, but halfway there I think that I am creating magical fantasy from my distress. I start to turn the car around. It will be too devastating when it doesn't work. I believe in good outcomes but this seems impossible. I will go home.

I don't turn the car around after all. Life can only offer me what I am open to receiving. I've got fifteen minutes till the SPCA closes for the weekend. I've got cash in my pocket for Jessie's SPCA fees, a carton with two dozen assorted cans of California Naturals in the back seat, and a heart that feels like a race-car driver is tracking through it. There's an old Dodge Dart in front of me traveling slow. Another car growls and speeds past. I trust in you, God. I'm opening my mind to all this. You gotta pull it through. Make this all real. I've got a heart to protect. It's beating strong and loud in my chest. It's my truest gemstone. Don't break it. Help.

I switch on the right turn signal and pass the driver who is coasting. We will do it together. We will pull this reality through. Come on, Jessie. Come on, God. We're a trio now. Let's go. Green light. I'm up to 25 miles an hour through the city. Green light. I'm up to 30. There's a cop in my back window. Suddenly he's there. It's always suddenly. It's right when you think you're getting somewhere. He turns on his siren. He flashes his light. He whooshes past me and is a block ahead ten seconds later. Bingo! Another green light. I'm back to 25. Thirteen minutes. Let's do it safely. Another green one and I'm on Seventh Avenue in Live Oak, the street where the SPCA building is located.

This is the magic that is going to work. This is the intention that is going to manifest. This day will turn my trust into something very deep. I'm in the parking lot. I'm parking the car.

I bring Shadow home. In the car I have Shadow in the carrier while Jessie is clearly next to me, bodiless in the air. Uh oh.

Back home with Shadow, and my boyfriend being out of town is evident in the house. I miss him. He gently affirms who I am when he is near. I feel very seen and appreciated by him

He is smooth. I feel like a cushion on a couch with him. Shadow is under the bed. His black and white fluffy body is handsome against the the white comforter behind him. I prepare myself for life with a quiet cat unlike my Jessie Boy, the talker. My home smells like vanilla. The tree branches dance outside. Still, the sound in the silence is clogged with emptiness. The air is stretched thin with disappointment.

    Gina had said that it may take months and maybe years for Jessie to become recognizable in his new body. She said that animals who reincarnate sometimes percolate back in bit by bit. Perhaps? But there is a kind cat under my bed who is a stranger. Perhaps we will remain separate strangers for the next six months, if not forever.

    Somehow, I just accept it. The moon is out again. I trust the moon. Maybe this will be a lesson in patience. I'm okay. I'm calm. I'm half a note away on the musical scale from downward travel into sorrow. C sharp. B flat. It's all the same. Be natural. I'm lost. I'm crying. I'm a faucet that can't seem to be turned off. But I sit in patience. I deepen into my own cells. The thoughts I think fill up with the nectar of acceptance, and I am bathed by what I exude. I am at last saturated in peace. I give up and rest in myself.

"Don't continue to look for Jessie's body" both of the cat communicators had told me after his disappearance. "If Jessie wishes to be seen, he will be."

Four hours later, to my surprise, Shadow begins to turn into Jessie Boy right before my eyes. He jumps on the bed. He purrs, turns in a little circle, and plops his back firmly against my chest and face to nap, just like Jessie!! His initial timidity is turning into Jessie's strength. As Shadow he was taciturn and cautiously looked around. As Jessie, he is in charge without needing an invitation. His eye contact changes dramatically to resemble Jessie's. His fear of noises turns to Jessie Boy's courage. He hisses at a big animal he sees outside. The body language changes dramatically! He is in charge. His tail is straight up in the air with enthusiasm. His ears are up and listening.

Soon he rubs my cheek with his. Jessie Boy is incarnating back home, far more himself than I had expected! I feel the deepest eternal space of endless love and peace that I have ever encountered. I am merged with Jessie. I am taken into a place of Heaven with Jessie. I am shown a world of no beginning or ending where all is one. For hours we are in another realm. It's angelic. It's bright. It's sweet. Everything is taken care of. It's Heaven on Earth, and my cat is showing me that it's possible. There are realms to find right here. I am formless, timeless, and One Love merged with Jessie.

"Jessie wants you to know that he won't be exactly the same. He will have gone through some changes. He's worried that you might expect him to have exactly the same mannerisms and look, but it may not be that way," Gina had said.

"Ask him if he will still cuddle with me a lot of the time."

"Cuddling is our expertise" was Jessie's answer.

I had asked Gina to tell Jessie to look deep into my eyes if he returned, as that is the only way I could imagine recognizing his essence. He does. The eyes that once held Shadow's soul fill up with that Jessie adoration and love look. It is Jessie. I recognize him. He looks into my eyes for an hour, filling me with warmth and expansive sweet energy. This is very unusual for a feline. He calms my turbulent aqua doubt into pale blue-sky faith. We melt into timeless spaceless. There is not more me or him or anyone but All. From this day on, I will remember my foundation in this one neutral love out of which all forms arise and fall endlessly to experience union, aloneness, reunion, and play.

In the instant of a thought, a half-consciously chosen change of channel, bundled up in my fluffy white comforter, listening to the crickets through the window screen, I am back in the awareness of myself as an individual and Jessie as a separate individual. Moving the inner flashlight from the beauty to a thought, I am immediately pulled back into the realm of separation

This too is a gift. All is. Jessie and I bring the light with us. Life is soft now. Content to sit in life's lap, I am elated.

He meows when I say "Jessie Boy," in that unique uplifting "mirrrrorrr" noise he has always used. This miracle on Earth delights me beyond what I expected. Jessie is home. At this time my heart is open so wide that my mind has no doubts. My heart has filled up my body and the room. My heart and Jessie's are one song singing thank you to life! Jessie and Shadow are magic! Thank you both.

Twelve Hours Later

Jessie Justin Joy (his new name) begins to demonstrate the old quirks. A nip on my ankle means the food is not acceptable: It must be the Wellness flavor or nothing. The old scratching routine gets me laughing. When I scratch his chin, he scratches my arm. He is a master soccer player just like last time. He will not leave my side hour after hour in order to assure me that it is him! He jumps behind the desk to unplug the computer when I spend too much time working. With his previous body he could do that. In his new body he isn't as large and doesn't have the strength, but he shows me that he's trying.

When people arrive for the workshop they assume he's my long-term pal. When I mention that he moved in just last night, everyone is shocked. "You two seem like you have been together forever!" Divine celebration has its own mind and I tell the story, forgetting that people might think this Doctor of Expressive Arts Psychology is crazy. Instead people cry. One man who has a New York accent and the enthusiasm of a puppy says how touched he is that I would share such a beautiful event with them. He tells us a story about seeing his dog's soul vividly in the backyard after his dog died.

My feline companion is fully Jessie, but his energy is even more powerful. He has filled me up with light. I am not the same at all. I find a happiness that goes far beyond emotion. Emotional happiness comes and goes. Joy from the source is eternal and available under any and all circumstances. All I need to do is tune to it in the moment, each moment. I am at peace. I am in joy. The green couch feels like marshmallows. My thoughts, often jagged and uneven, become velvet sounds.

Friends come over, recognizing and commenting that our boy is back with a new body. Home is full of grinning and smiling. He is beautiful, the color of Oreo cookies.

Ray is delighted to see him. "Can you tell it's him?" I ask. Some people aren't able to recognize him, but others know right away. One of my students, Jeri, says, "That's him. He came straight to the door to greet me as always."

"I can't tell, Love, maybe he is." Ray always speaks his truth in a way that puts me at ease and validates my experience. Ray gets on the floor with Jessie Boy Justin Joy and pets him, saying, "Welcome home, Sweetheart."

A Month Later

This incarnation, my feline angel and I have a graceful, easy cheer about us. Jessie is very calm, and whenever he expresses a need, desire, or want with bold strength he follows it up with a cuddle to assure me that love is always present. He makes it clear that he will not be going to the vet. I can call Dr. Blake, the homeopathic Western-trained vet, but he wants no car rides to the animal clinic where he spent far too much time last incarnation. The final years of his last life were full of doctors, medicines, and operations. This time his body is fully healthy. He leaps and jumps each time I try to put him into the carrier, then runs to kiss me. If I try again he leaps and jumps away like a bunny.

I am a new person. I have committed to going by the rules of spirit instead of ego/world. That fiery question that revved up my days and plagued my nights—"How can I succeed?"—has been reshaped to "How can I live in love, devotion, joy, openness in each moment?" Jessie guides me well with every client, each momentary choice, my personal life, so I listen. I respect him as a divine teacher as well as a divine partner/learner and take all of his communications with great respect. He points me to the source of what is valuable during each life encounter.

Jessie helps me to live in a world where all is well. With his guidance I seek happiness in the infinite instead of the circumstances. Jessie keeps me on track, quieting my restless mind with strong presence. He puts his paw gently on my face. He licks my hand. He massages my head. Ray notices that I am changing and he holds me. He swims with me like water. He seems to know how I am deep inside, so outer changes are very easy for him. He likes who I am. I feel very at home.

Two Months Pass
Jessie's gaze is looking like it used to in that tiger body he once lived in. The Jessie expression and eyes are back. He's become a BIG fluffy guy now with a huge lion mane all around his face and chest. His tail is full and lovely. He's chirping away when he feels delighted in EXACTLY the same Jessie accents he used in his last body! I used to call him Tiger Man. Now his nickname is Little Lion.

Ray, Jessie, and I are very happy with each other. Jessie in his tiger body warned me about boyfriends prior to this one and was right when he said, "No go." He identified my Love right away as "the one we had been waiting for." Now, two years later, I see that Jessie was right. I am with the love I have always needed and desired. Jessie can look very deeply into a person's soul and see them. He is my helper, my friend, and my teacher. He is far more evolved than I, so I tune into him and get to go to realms of bright light, master's blessings, and bliss.

Jessie inspires me to discover that real joy includes all circumstances as they are. Inner joy is not dependent upon life being one way or another. It is a feeling of unconditional love for all that is just as it is in the heart. Real joy is happiness that exists at all times as long as I choose to be aware of it. Real joy sings consistently in late-summer night air, swimming in my chest. I am learning that it is okay to be happy because it's my preference. I am discovering that I can be happy just because I was made to be so. No specific reason is needed. All causes attributed to happiness bloom and wilt, while true joy remains forever.

I am happier than I have ever been. A client says, "You are so happy because your cat came back." I am happy because my cat came back and brought a part of myself with him—a part that I must have left behind many years ago.

Cats are supposedly aloof, but my boy likes to be rocked like a baby until he sleeps. He also likes to be held and snuggled like a teddy bear all night! He likes to be by my side almost every moment that I am home. We find out that he is a rag doll breed. His long-haired black tail is adorned with one white stripe down the middle. He has an auburn Saturn-like ring around his upper body. When he jumps up from a nap, straightens his ears, looks out the window and growls, I know that another animal is near. But when a very nervous two-pound kitten runs into our home and attacks Jessie Justin Joy, he just comforts her lovingly. He is my role model. I celebrate his teachings and existence with gratitude!

I feel very safe in life. I know I will always have my friend with me forever, for all eternity. For all lifetimes. And I ask God to keep Ray with me forever also. There is no abandonment to fear. It has been dissolved. Shortly after his reincarnation, Jessie Justin Joy, Ray, and I moved into a new home together.

Ray has been hesitant about sharing a home with an indoor cat. After a few weeks Ray tells me about his men's group.

"'I have a surprise,' I told the guys this evening," Ray says. "I have a new member of my family. He's a cat. Jessie is so sweet. I love him. Living with him is a delight! He is my feline son." Every morning Jessie Justin Joy walks and runs up and down the long steep driveway doing my aerobic routine with me. When Ray opens the door to the stairs, he runs up and plops himself on his back in front of Ray's feet, knowing he will receive a massage. I trust the magic of the universe. Jessie Justin Joy teaches me unconditional love and joy day by day.

Yellow-Winged Moth Ushers in Love and Peace

As a therapist I make appearances as a public speaker. One of my favorite topics is "Practices to Create Success in Joy." One year I am the Keynote Speaker for the Women in Business Expo put on by the *Santa Cruz Sentinel*. As I am getting ready to head to the podium, a beautiful yellow-winged moth lands on my books.

"Are you here to speak with me?" I ask.
"Yes, I have come to assist with your talk."
"What do you wish for me to know?"

"The information you impart at your talk is secondary. It's good for people to hear about the topic but that is not your PRIMARY purpose. The reason you have been called to give this talk is to be in peace. As you stand in the vibration of unconditional peace, so too will the audience."

"Okay," I agree with great gratitude. The moth and I arrange to be in each other's hearts throughout the talk. As I give the talk I am in peace.

After the talk, many doubts evaporate from my consciousness. I feel certain that my entire life has been used well, that I have made right decisions for my necessary learning--even the errors. I have given my contributions and amends, while everything has come in valuable order. I am doing what I agreed to do on Earth as an imperfect, vulnerable, well-meaning, and powerful human. This is a huge relief inside me, as I have frequently been full of goals and ambitions, chronically feeling that I fall short!

Yellow-winged moth invites me to discover that my purpose is to BE love. Yellow-winged moth helps me to know that I am doing this to the best of my ability. This is success. My moth beloved brings me contentment.

After the speech I return to my chair. My moth friend is gone. Several minutes later she flies over to me, seemingly out of nowhere, landing on my arm! We look at each other in awe and gratitude. Her little eyes are precious.

"Thank you, my love," says my friend, yellow-winged moth, to me.

"Thank you, my love," I say to the little one.

Two bugs appear. Away fly the three.

I am taken to profound peace that lasts. My life is forever changed. I am invited to live in the unconditional. Of course I accept the invitation!

Each second invites us to live in the unconditional. You may focus so fully on physical sensations, emotional waves, and descriptive words that you melt back into the source of all existence. Uni-Verse, whose source of all

existence. Uni-Verse, whose one song holds all beings in many flavors, with many faces, loves you. The birth and death of this second is an opportunity for subtracting what is no longer needed. This makes room for a blooming surrender to love that is vast and kind.

Red-Tail Hawk Day

We fall asleep with the window open. We like to sleep entwined, all three, resting in a shared heartbeat. I felt the spirits beckon me outside. I am as outside as I can be while my body relaxes into the bed with my family. There is a song in the air. The tones of bass, tenor, alto, and soprano are cooperating.

The night becomes my lover, holding me. I am in love, cradled in my entirety. Night wraps me up like a soft lavender blanket as my skin feels nourished. I feel nourished to the core. Mesmerized by the sweet scent held out to me as a gift from the wild ginger, I seep into the night. I am pulled home like a child to a father's chest, by the love peering through the gleaming eyes of the sky, the stars. Ray's soothing energy is wrapped into the night too. Jessie Justin Joy's heart leaps like sparks in the air. I remember that all that matters to me is to follow this divine love. In action and in complete stillness, this love has me fully.

When morning peers through the window, the mountains promise that I am them. "You will be a strong warrior, as strong as we are if you feed yourself well. Take good care of your body. Eat good food. Eat our strength through your gaze." As I listen, I breathe in the rich greens that cover the hills. Memory slides through consciousness of a time during which I was an Indian boy. I wondered if it was my soul that lived an Indian boy's life. Perhaps the memory arises from something else. Maybe there is an Indian boy in my ancestral line, recorded in my DNA. Letting the question grow into thought, then fade with breath, I remain in love.

Day begins. I am showered, dressed, now walking up and down the hill. I have been feeling very tired from the output of energy over the last couple of weeks, and the walk is rejuvenating. Feline JJJ doesn't do as many laps as I do, so he chooses to wait at the bottom of the hill after we share three. A grapefruit hangs low from the small tree, catching my eye. I walk over to pick it. "Thank you," I say to the little bush.

As I thank the tree, this heart is filled with his warmth. The tree emanates "thank you" in return. Sharing this gratitude, I feel complete.

Lime green, evergreen, dark green, and pastel green surround me.

The phone rings through the window. I go back inside to answer. Reality shifts. Someone calls about an argument they just had with their spouse. The person's voice scratches against me. I feel as though the two of us are C# and D on the phone, silently competing. I want her to feel happier while she asks me to feel her pain. I suggest she stop in to receive some support and create some relief in a couple of days Back outside, doing laps up and down the hill, I am complaining to myself: "I need more energy. What happened? The hawks have been gone for almost a week."

Then he flies in front of me. His name is Red-Tail Hawk. He has beautiful wings and big feet. My heart relaxes into the lingering resistance to the C# and D disharmonic where I release into harmony. I watch him go straight in front, next up to the sky, circling to my right. His pink, gray, and red colors carry my heart up into the sky with him. I am on the ground and I am flying at the same time. "Come here, if you would," I request. "Would you teach me how to be stronger?"

At once he tends to me, circling closely above. Loud buzzing sounds begin. The dragonflies arrive. Three of them come to dance by me as I watch the hawk. The sun pats my forehead. I stretch my arms out as I look up. He is now straight above me, still for a moment, with his wings also stretched.

"Thank you, thank you. What does life ask of me?" I query.

"We ask that you be very quiet, content, and listen to us. We are stronger than you can imagine and we have a message for you now. Come back to us."

I look down where I find two little ladybugs making love. The universe is rich with helpers and lovers.

"Please teach me to be a real servant," I say.

"A medicine woman of your type uses holy scriptures and objects to woo others back into their own flight ... back to themselves beyond you ... back to who they are."

"Yes, and I am doing a good job?"

"There's more. Go deeper. When we are missing from your gaze, you must go deeper to call us back in gently. When you don't see us, go further into your own magic. Then watch how quickly we return." Red-Tail is now gone, but a vision of him above a lake appears, blaring kindly and alarmingly into my mind. He looks like he is swooping down lower.

"You still give too much of yourself away," he cautions. I hear him though his body is no longer visible. I rub my palm with my other hand, feeling the different muscles all doing their jobs in one hand.

"How do I know what limits and boundaries to set?"

"Be more careful. Spend more time with us and you will learn. It's your turn."

"What can I offer you in return?"

"You can only offer yourself. There is nothing more and nothing less."

"What do I do next?"

"You must sit by a creek and let us come through the back door. It is our time to come to you."

I start making plans to drive out to Felton and visit Fall Creek. I stop in my own tracks, recalling something I had read in a book by

Raymon Grace. He said you can connect to the water anywhere, from wherever you are. Instead of getting in the car, going to the gas station, and driving a ways, I send my soul to the creek from where I am.

Now I hear chimes and high-pitched sounds. A cool breeze smiles both at me and in me, causing my heart to relax. I lie on the ground, feeling massaged by the sun, collected in the earth. I replenish.

"You have lost your soul memory. You are only halfway there. You must listen deeper. Listen to the night. Listen to the forest. Listen to the day. Listen to us and not to anyone else. We will help you. We are clear and we are in everything. Hear us."

I cry. "I am here, Mother of life. Here I am and I will run to you." JJJ runs to me now. "I will listen."

"Have you noticed that every song and dance, everything you do for us has always stayed with you and come back to you? There is no past that isn't here."

"Yes."

"Then soak your face in the creek. Be cared for. Be served."

I do. In the cooling water, my energy grows stronger. I see an image of an owl when I put my head under.

Bathed and nourished, held and supported, suddenly rejuvenated, I lie in the water. I have spent many occasions in water with my physical body: the creeks, the oceans, the rivers, and the lakes. Now, right from my house without going anywhere, I am fully relieved, cleansed and re-energized. The water has come to me.

"Thank you to the water all over the planet!" I celebrate out loud. "You are the life within us all. I love you forever. You are my hero. Thank you. May you be loved by everyone forever. I send you my love and I find myself home in you."

I feel Red-Tail Hawk and Owl alive in my being. Flaming strength has been lit in my heart. My feet are alive and wise as they feel the clay-baked earth. Hearing
the message Red-Tail Hawk sends to Earth, I am saturated in faith. I sit down in a soft outdoor chair, astounded that I can go from burnt out and lifeless to fully strong in an hour. It is in letting them guide me. It is in letting the hawk

and the guides take me that strength comes from my source. There is no more strength in anything I do alone. It must come from the guidance of the wise ones.

JJJ sits under the chair I sit in. We breathe. Contentment blends with a strand of awe. Love tangoes with the laughter streaming through the air. A neighbor turns on a very loud motorcycle, passing us in a blurry gray uproar, down the hill, around, and back up.

We stay close to the ground, held by equanimity's grace. I send love to the neighbor. He is expressing himself in the way that he chooses. All is intriguing in the contrasts of sounds. There is room for us both in our different modes. I hear the canyon echo back to him.

"RRrr," says the motorcycle.

"RRrr," says the canyon.

"WOORP!" shouts the motorcycle. "WOORP!" shouts the canyon. My heart is amazed at how powerful our messages are. What we sing, sings back. JJJ and I are being held in the life mirror. I laugh. He blinks his eyes as a soft smile.

Neighbors approach our shared driveway. I decide to camouflage myself the way JJJ does. I cannot talk and simultaneously maintain this strength of silence.

I lie on my back on the ground between the shrubs and vines. JJJ remains with me. I make myself flat and still.

"Thanks for coming all the way up here," I hear one say to another.

"It's a miracle I didn't barf," his friend replies in response. Why do I have neighbors whose miracles are stuff like this?

I remembered what Gina told me: "Anyone who shows up in your reality is there because you called them there." I chuckle silently.

I am growing stronger. Something is brewing inside me. This feels stronger than anything I have ever known myself to be before. I am feeling the hawk and the owl in my muscles and blood in a most present, awe-inspiring, and enlivening way. I realize that the neighbor and his friend have the hawk and the owl in them also. We share this energy. Red-Tail and Owl are full of us. The sun carries everyone.

When the humans pass, the energy lessens, affirming that being together makes life more powerful. No experience is solely mine alone. I feel more respect
There is something to learn about the judgments that have arisen silently between us over time. There is something better beckoning us. Red-Tail Hawk is calling this forth.

JJJ and I remain in the silence. Suddenly Red-Tail Hawk flies right over me. JJJ is under a chair. I am open to the sky though camouflaged on the sides of my body. Red-Tail Hawk is only a few feet above with a red beak.

JJJ runs. I am taken over by complete feminine love. This hawk must be a female. I sit up quickly to protect JJJ, then notice that he has run from under the chair to the open and is hunting. Is JJJ safe?

Fear thoughts erupting from my belly disrupt the smooth, complete, vast and safe love.

"Will you keep JJJ safe?" I ask both Red-Tail Hawk and life itself.

"There are only thoughts of love and thoughts of fear. Your thoughts choose realities," is the answer that comes back.

Hours pass. The day is getting ready to come to a close. Time to turn into the night. With great grace and smoothness one becomes the other. JJJ sits safely on the deck with the loving sun filtering from his yellow eyes into the world. I slip inside to put a load of towels in the washing machine.

"Go down to the deck behind the house," I hear Red-Tail Hawk speak, though I do not see him.

Maybe JJJ and I should go for round three of lessons with Red-Tail Hawk I think to myself.

"There is no reason to do that" Red-Tail hears me. "Always follow your instincts. Your instincts tell you to go to the back deck, so there you shall go." I go to the back deck where I lie in a chair. I feel that love is coming from me and love is coming to me. All the love that ever was in the universe is having a reunion with her/himself in me. I am no one but everyone, and this can be happening in all who allow.

"Our work today is complete," Red-Tail Hawk gently offers. "Listen to the message of now." She is gone.

I am enveloped in perfect love. All is complete. The day is right on track, knowing exactly what is supposed to have happened. Everything is in its right time and place. I feel perfect love. My job is done just as it needed to be done. What I yearn for is here now.

A couple of days earlier, a client named Jake came in. He told me that a woman was caustic to him, screaming at him when he has been loving and kind. He confuses himself by still feeling attached to her. I feel he is telling the truth. I sense he has been very kind.

He told me of his land called "Two Grandmothers" because two grandmother spirits live there. They often walk by him, one on each side, at night, with great love. He told me of the hummingbirds who fly around his face with great love and his friends the ravens. His visit to my office was a blessing, informing me that the world is changing.

I told him that it is harder to let go of someone who is mean to us than someone who is just not a good fit. This is because the soul yearns for resolution that is kind. When there is none the personality feels a desire to go back and solve it.

"So close your eyes," I said to the kind man, "and imagine a woman that you will meet in the future. You can feel her now. This woman will love you with great love and kindness like the love and kindness you give. She will love you like the hummingbirds and the grandmothers. From now on, when your mind focuses on the woman who hurt you, immediately shift your mind to the woman who will love you. You will find her this way, first inside yourself and then outside."

I know he can realize this potential. It is how I found Ray. Jake has great love in his heart to surrender to creation's artistry, the yang and the yin in cooperation.

Suddenly, while lying on the chair on the deck in perfect love, I feel this man and his two grandmothers sending me so much love that I cry. All the years of feeling that my work was not worthy enough fades. I am helping people in real ways. All my complaining that I was tired is now washed away, transformed into light-blue sky which blankets my heart tenderly, fills my eyes with complete nourishment. Many beautiful souls hold me in gratitude in their hearts. Everything is and will always be tended to.

I am about to get up and go inside when I hear a noise. A sparrow lands right in my gaze. "Hello, sweet bird," I say. He looks at me, preening himself for a while. I realize that my job is not complete.

"Guides of mine and guides of all my clients I ever met, I send this message now. You are held in the arms of the Divine Mother and you are forever loved. All is well in your worlds," I say aloud.

Now I hear the great wail. Reverberating throughout is a deep-seated big sob from the pit of the stomach that lives in the world. I hold this sob in my arms like a baby, cover him in a blanket, rock her back and forth while I articulate, "You are loved now forevermore. Hear this today. Dial them up. Wake them up. Please, get their attention any way you can," I ask birds and spirits. "Help them."

"We are doing all we can. Now it is your humanity that must listen."

I remembered what radio interviewer Marsha Morgan told me on the air. She said that a hawk came to visit and took a bath in her bird bath just a foot away from her and they were immediate friends. I feel appreciation for Marsha. And I think gratefully of Gina teaching her class to people so they can hear animals more clearly. I realize that so many of us are in love with animals and life now that everyone can catch on.

So I listen deep into the love that the birds have woven into the sky and continue.

Jonah the Awakened Dove

During four decades I long. One day Jonah the dove sits on my shoulder. He whispers, "If you want to be content, be content. It's easy." Then I realize, as I melt into the love, that I am content. I had simply forgotten. The light I had shined on the struggle was held by a content source. Now my heart melts into this source of contentment, which holds me home.

Jonah the dove appears as a six-ounce enlightened master who is fully protected from anything that is not light. Simultaneously he is without boundaries in his relationship to the light. After many years of studying closely with a variety of human gurus, I encounter Jonah. In silence and through the heart, Jonah takes me to a place of eternal bliss, light, and love. I entered this place three years back when Jessie Justin Joy, my feline, reincarnated. At that time I remembered and entered a realm in which there is only one time and one space. Now, sitting with Jonah, all thought is removed from my head, letting me exist in forever-expanding light and sound, gleeful and ecstatic.

Many of you readers are blessed to hear trees sing in eternity, the angelic choir offer lullaby, or the eternal tones that add choir to the forest. Until my meeting with Jonah, I experienced entrance into this realm as a come-and-go gift. Jonah shows me that I can be in this place of light at any time I choose simply by putting my focus here inside. Outside now reveals itself to emanate from inside. Inside shows itself to be made of outside.

Jonah travels with Divine Mother, Jesus, Buddha, angels, and archangels. "Who is your main teacher?" I ask him. Jonah showed me that his main teacher is vast light that expands forever ... the sun and the moon as one ... love that goes on eternally.

"You are in my heart forevermore," Jonah tells me. I spend many hours with him, holding him on my lap when we are in physical proximity. I share meetings with him from miles away, when our bodies are parted. Jonah lives in eternity everywhere.

Jonah helps me to know that the quickest route to ascend is to connect to my own light source. Since our first contact, daily life has been a series of beautiful awakenings into unconditional contentment, love, joy, and peace. Of course, this is a practice. Sometimes I remember and sometimes I forget. Each forgetting is an invitation. I am asked by life to face more of my ego aspects, allowing these to be removed, apologizing to source for their appearance, making way for the next unconditional experience and the next set of ego appearances.

Jonah shows me how easy it is to release individual and collective karmic ego aspects. Psychological introspection is fine. It is the long route, and scenes may be delightful or miserable depending upon the degree of attachment you have to them. Grace is the Heavenly scenic highway! Call it in, for your heart is opened by this calling. Ascendance is free to all. Make it your intention to be love, to be honest about anything in you that is not love, and allow all but love to dissolve.

Now is the time for instant manifestation. The masters are teaching us that whatever we focus upon magnifies. Our intention is flavored by the quality we practice. If we practice trust, life appears trustworthy. If we allow compassion, life is full of compassion. Whatever your intention is made of qualitatively will become your experience immediately in this new day and age. You choose to study ego attachment and misery or love-light. Your personal experience will be the reflection of your choices. However, in the light, you and all your choices are loved and forgiven, recognized only as sound and light in motion, held forever in the arms of Divine Mother and beings of the ONENESS such as Jonah.

Discussions with Animal Teachers

When I am in despair, confusion, or doubt, wisdom from the animals' worlds brings me back to trust in unconditional love, joy, and peace. Each animal-being responds to a question from his or her own soul-calling. Individuals have their own perspectives.

The following messages are from animal volunteers who offered to assist in this process. The question asked is "What is the most important focus for humans during this century?"

Jonah the Dove

"Very happy you ask me. White Light. Pray for birds. Birds feed goodness to humanity in struggle. Sit. Listen. The sounds will help guide you to the guides. We are free in our hearts. Our answers are in whispers. You can hear in air when quiet. Light is Light. Life is Light. You are free when you know all about us. Pure light is the real world. It is here."

Jessie the Feline

Cause and Effect. Be aware of your intentions. Each thought you think gives a lesson in instant reality that you create. Each challenge is the result of a repeated thought. Think wisely to avoid bad karma. Instant enlightenment is available through unconditionally chosen joy, peace, and love. The intention to know these unconditional realms creates favorable circumstances. Trust us when we speak to you. When we *prrrr* and sit close or watch you intently, it is with a message for you. Listen very carefully to your heart when a feline is near for s/he is helping you to reach your ultimate destiny: pure satisfaction.

Charcoal Beauty the Canine

Oh, you came back! Humanity, you have chosen us and we have chosen you! Listen with all your heart, for the eternal white light is shining everywhere. It is in you. You are it. The dog follows the master because the real master is trust and devotion. We will help you. We will climb mountains if it takes that to bring you home. You are one of us and we are one of you.

Whales

Vast One. Ripples are the dreams of devotion.

Dolphins

Yep! Play. Bop up and down in a bibbity bop, people! Golden light is coming to transform you. Smile. We are your ancestors. Our energy changes you from the insideout. We celebrate golden light swimming into the meridians of the humans who choose. There are no mistakes. The time is right for us to enter your spirits. We love you. We play games in duality. For ultimate trust, come closer so we may help you. Self-defeating habits are melting. Playing is here to be used for incredible joy and play. Release it! It's gone. Love. Forgive! Be the enjoying! Everyone is forgiven foreverything forever. We're here and we embrace you with glee!

Psychotherapy with Two Doves

A very feminine, fully white dove arrives in the spirit realm. I know that an animal-being is contacting me when he or she appears very close up in a photo image in my mind. The images will always take a gentle hold of my heart, gathering me into a feeling of happiness and alertness. When an animal is choosing to come and speak to me, her photo image is presented first, followed immediately by her essence zooming in. I differentiate this from a dream of which I am the primary author. When I include animals and other guides in dreams that I write, they take on my essence. When they come to me and invite me to enter their dream, they make their unique essence very clear for me to feel.

After I am approached by an animal in the spiritual dimension, he will often show up in the physical dimension days, months, or even years later. A canine comes to me to say that he will protect me. He also communicates that he will teach me to better protect myself. I feel this round-faced and sturdy, big brown fellow with a bit of black highlights to be nearby. I ask around to see if he lives with anyone I know. No one recognizes the description. I look but cannot find him anywhere outside the spirit world.

Some months later I am on a walk with my partner Ray when I see the dog staring at me with great fondness. He sits in the distance in the physical realm. I recognize his face, body, and energy at once. Delightful! I can feel his presence now as I write about him. This fills me with great joy. Lessons that come from the animals are not always translatable to my rational mind, but they forever take me deeper into states of present time, joy, and a wholehearted appreciation for being.

Some animals that greet me in the spirit realm tell me that I will not be finding them in physical form, but I will reunite with them in similar form after my incarnation here. We will be in other dimensions together. Others call from long distance requesting help. Often I invite all masters of deepest love, goodness, and highest teachings to approach me. Prior to Satsang we hold meetings. The house becomes full of many beings from the sea, the earth, and the sky. As I lie in bed early in the morning, a white feminine dove appears.

"It's me. Sara."

Am I mistaken? Sara is a white dove who had been master teacher Dove Spirit's true love and soul mate. Spirit is Jonah's father from a current marriage. Sara had

a short life span. She passed away.

"No, it's ME, Sara. Spirit and I still have work to do together on other planes."

Although I didn't fully understand, the birds make it clear to me that Spirit and his current wife are very much connected here in the physical world at their home in California. Sara and Spirit remain in union in another realm of infinity.

"Come along now." Sara and Spirit are showing me how to fly. As sweet clear breath washes through this body, breeze moves through my lungs. Cleansed and sailing in clear energy, I am refreshed.

A prayer asking to be given deeper cleansing tools is being answered in living motion.

Traveling into ecstatic realms, I go to my office, where I enter an unexpected healing crisis. I fall asleep in the office chair. When I rise, I am full of toxic energy. I have let emotional debris from people in valuable catharsis get into my body. Opened-hearted, I have taken in too much.

At home, I bathe but the water does not reach deep enough inside me. I fall asleep holding a rock gifted to me from a dear friend. Rock and intention purify me while I ask for guidance. Now, guidance is here. Another prayer is answered.

Flying within myself in the protection and clear clean energy of Sara, I am air. There are no more words. I let all words of the mind drop from my body the way that birds poop into the earth, so what is not needed will be composted. I release thinking to feel the clear clean air moving through me. I become the air with Spirit and Sara by my side.

An hour later, I begin to think again, spinning into extra realities of mind, losing focus, falling into dizziness. Energy in my body is wobbling as though I am fizzling out.

"This is how you get sick and pick up unnecessary energy," Sara explains. "When you forget that your focus is Great Spirit Wind, making the client's circumstances your focus instead, your world-center wobbles. Toxins come in, and you feel ill instead of feeling your harmony with all that is. Free harmony is still there to gather you up when you focus on it. So refocus and spread yourself into the winds. Feel how you fly."

I feel my soul flowing into the air, brushing by trees. Wonder and awe of life feed my being, tingling ecstatically in my bones, muscles, and blood. Feeling quick mastery of the lesson, I am suddenly concerned that the bird friends will go. I will be left alone.

They settle in my belly as they show themselves perching on tree branches. "We are always here with you, and learning is forever yours," they assure me.

The next lesson is how to blend in deeper harmony with my partner, Ray. When we first met, the mutual intrigue was so strong that we naturally worked as a collaborative team. We had a magic way of blending into each other as though there were one of us. Now we often have our individual rhythms going in our home. On busier days, while we are both very involved in individual projects, we merge less. As we are always aware of each other in the house, a deeper peace that is solid exists within all the movement. At the same time, I find myself frustrated by not knowing how to blend more often. Sometimes I am so immersed in my own projects that I can't remember how to harmonize with Ray's waves of energy.

Sara and Spirit have me up in the air. I realize that they are giving me the visceral awareness of how to do a fly-by. When a bird wants to know someone she will fly close to that person and feel the energy that person is emitting. Spirit says that I can return to union with Ray at any moment I choose if I sensitize my energy to his energy with a fly-by.

This is how Spirit's lesson converts to the human body: I focus on my partner to feel his energy, remaining aware of the feeling of my own energy. Next I walk closer to where he is while allowing the energies to naturally mingle, finding a way to merge. Once the energies have settled into a well-mixed blend I can make physical contact if I feel like it. This practice can be done in the garden, during a conversation, when making love, on the phone, while cleaning the house, and in endless other situations. It's easy and simple, as my teachers Sara and Spirit show me. Thank you, my dear friends and master guides! This kind of psychotherapy is quick, fun, and positive. It is my cup of tea. These birds are highly evolved beings and teachers of the light, the union, and the harmonious ways to experience duality.

Shera, a Feline Healer

My feline friend Shera is a skilled healer. Shera unexpectedly arrives in my office in the spirit realm when I become suddenly ill. Last we met was in body at her home in Carlsbad, California. I have eaten a burrito from a restaurant and am now experiencing cramps in my stomach that are so intense I can barely stand. It's time to leave the office but I cannot drive. I feel too sick to cross the room to call Ray.

    I try to force myself to the bathroom because I need to throw up, but I am too uncomfortable to move. A jagged stab is in my torso. Suddenly I am not thinking about the pain. I no longer know that this is what I call "pain." I am simply feeling, listening, and being alive as the sensation in my stomach. Waves of life are occurring while some light from deep within perceives this. The light simultaneously perceives many beings of many universes. The light makes this clear by shining reality through this heart.

    Shera shows me how to be fully present in my body, so individually present that "I" melt into this vast seeing. As a human I can exist in realms of thought while my body does all kinds of things. I can even go to dance class with my body but float off into dreams. Shera shows me that separating my mental existence from my physical is of no use to animals, nor to me. An animal will lose his/her life in the outdoors if consciousness is anywhere outside of the here, now, flesh.

What I did not know until this moment is that being completely present in the physical dissolves this being into an awareness of all holding the physical. This world is composed of motion in which each being is a series of waves. Each soul is a light form in which each wave generates. Nobody is separate.

As I feel each cell in my body, contentment floods this heart. The experience of fully inhabiting a body far outweighs anything more fulfilling I can think of in this second. I prefer pleasure, but in complete acceptance of the present, pain and pleasure cease to be important. Whatever exists is valuable. All notions of good/bad, better/worse, proud to be/embarrassed about, and other apparent opposites become useless. There is nothing to judge while fulfillment of living in the physical dimension is to fully inhabit it. In doing so I am simultaneously alive in many other dimensions, melting. What was known as pain is now revealed to be resistance. With the absence of resistance, only sensation occurs. Sensation left unmeasured and labeled simply is life.

Master animal guides are aware of this. Their physical, mental, and spiritual bodies are working as one. Thoughts are used to serve or express this process. Shera introduced me into this awareness. Thoughts from this type of existence are used solely to serve the needs of the present. There is no reason for analysis or explanation. "Know what is needed and respond," Shera prompts me.

Shera continues guiding me to transport myself fully into the cells of my body. What was intense pain becomes a sensation-experience. It is neither pain nor pleasure. It just is. It isn't good or bad. I lose all judgment and shame for what is occurring in my body. In this acceptance, adjustments take place. As I follow Shera's guidance to simply be present, my body knows what to do to bring itself back toward harmony.*

I curl up in a big chair like a cat. I am pulled into a very deep and tranquil sleep, and when I wake, I feel profound peace in my stomach. I have shifted from feeling I was going to faint from intense pain to feeling calmness, bliss, and joy in my body, all in ninety minutes.

Now I better understand Jessie's experience on the day he had the insulin attack many years ago. Within a few hours he went from frolicking in the grass, to being on the verge of death in the animal hospital, to returning home and hunting. He remained in peace for the entire journey.

At a later date, I am lying on the ground at Shera's sanctuary-home in Carlsbad. While listening to music with Dove Jonah, I feel a bit out of body, somewhat ungrounded. I am again approached by Shera, this time in the physical. This time she offers me energetic balancing. Of her own initiative, Shera limps in from outside, in her very elderly form, choosing to make an altruistic journey instead of resting in the sun. She comes to lie on my feet, with fiery prana in her body, pulling the energy down my legs, through the bottoms of my feet, and back to the ground. In the most selfless, devoted of ways, she simply knows what to do and does that. She is a medicine woman of the highest intuition, integrity, and training.

I continue to enjoy pleasure, but I now know that pain and pleasure are of equal value in the realm of pure presence. I ask life to bring me pleasure (as this is what I like best). I also ask life to help me live in the present when disharmonies occur so that I may heal rather than hide the disharmonies.

These extremes are not necessary for learning the lessons of presence but they teach something very important. When I live in the full present, everything comes and goes just as it does. This is enough. Satisfaction runs through all. Recovery time is a physical experience to move through. As humans we have the option of separating from the experience itself, to the witness who examines. This option does not appear to bring the harmony, contentment, and trust that are available when we choose to fully embody present experience.

I find that Shera's way of existing is healing, bringing me deep into the wonder, awe, and trust of life. Her body-present ability wakes me up, giving me everything I need right in the moment. Thank you, medicine woman, Shera. You have been a Grandmother to me. Siamese, slender, and strong, you show up when I least expect you but most need you. When I am experiencing imbalance or illness, you arrive. You purposefully teach me lessons of healing. You view illness without judgment, analysis, or resistance, embracing illness and humanity, as a Divine Mother.

Please note that the author is sharing a personal experience. She advises people to use doctors, vets, and health practitioners to assist in the event of a medical challenge. She uses these types of assistance herself.

Hu Huuuu, Peace Chant of the Doves

After learning and reciting a variety of mantras from many different religions, I noticed that "Hu" is a common one. This sound carries meanings of God, truth, and love, according to various cultures.

One day, I am visiting Dove Spirit and his family in their house. Spontaneously, I turn to them to say, "Thank you for welcoming me and allowing me to be in your presence during this sacred time of the baby." Spirit, astounding saintly father, is nurturing the baby hour after hour. The baby's determined and focused mother, who introduces herself to me with a nickname of Fragrenca, flies closer to me when she hears this. Spirit turns to face me. Both Sprit and Fragrenca bow while they say *"Hu Huuu"* over and over. I am deeply touched.

Later that day I spend time with Spirit's adult son, Jonah. Dove Jonah bows while he *Hu Huuus* to many a being, even an inanimate object, which makes me laugh with delight. How unconditional his love is for everyone and everything! I just love him.

Now I like to walk around my house bowing and *Hu Huuuing,* recalling Spirit, Fragrenca, and Jonah. I find when I do this that I am overtaken by laughter and overwhelming bliss. I see flashes of white light, feel love that surges through my heart, and hear jubilant laughter in the air. I would recommend the *Hu Huuu* chant to anyone who values joy and laughter! Remember to sing out *Hu Huuu* to give your love to the world. This is the intention of *Hu Huuu!*

Cat Mentor Sno

Sno is a little three-pounder. She has pure white hair, light marble-blue eyes, a pink nose, and slightly pink ears. She is a very angelic being with a magical and divine soul. Upon meeting Sno in physical form, I remembered the trust with which I used to greet my human playmates in my very early years. I encountered friends with innocence and an egoless sense of oneness. This was so long ago I had forgotten. My heart spilled over in tears of gratitude when Sno brought me home to these types of feelings. Sno reached a paw to me, looking in my eyes for a long time. I hadn't realized that I had been searching for this soul memory. Longing and fullness merged inside my heart.

Sno taught me that I am Divine. We all are. She taught me to give my Divine nature complete focus. This delicate master feline lives in a magic palace of sparkling grace. She is an angel who remembers her origins consistently.

Months before I see her in body she visits me in spirit. I first encounter Sno in spirit in my office. Tactfully and playfully she climbs on both me and my client, removing and replacing rigid places in us with fun, playful joy. Months later when I meet her in body she is already deeply familiar.

Sno's person explains that Sno used to respond eagerly to the cuddles and adoration given to her by many. Recently her canine friend Charles passed on. He had been a father to Sno. She sat on his grave with her arms outstretched for four days, not eating, only mourning. Since then, she allows nobody to touch her or compliment her lovely appearance with the exception of her family. Others are snarled at.

I ask Sno about this. She explains that in her past, people pulled her out of the essence into more superficial posturing and interacting. She refuses to engage in these types of interactions now. People have to come deeply into their pure magic to meet her resonance. She will not budge to meet them in a less fulfilling arena of existence. Her commitment to this invites others to ascend into states of being fully connected to their source and their angels.

This makes an immense impression on me. How often I leave the temple of my existence to meet people in societally willed engagements, feeling deeply unsatisfied. I decide to stay in my temple too. From this decision life changes. Prayer and meditation deepen. Life becomes only prayer, intention, release, gratitude, and meditation. Friendships deepen while other friendships fade away. Many a moment becomes wondrous. Held by
my creator I am fulfilled, generating love that touches and completes.

Language is a Beautiful Tool for Expression, says Lizard

Are you understanding me? Am I hearing you? Am I making it all up?

Ray and I are walking when we come across a little lizard. Engrossed in eye contact, I tell the lizard I love her. Swept into doubt, I ask, "Are we really communicating?"

Little Lizard scurries over to me. She travels up my body to my back. She stays with Ray and me for a good fifteen minutes while we walk. Language is the riverbed for the water that connects us all. My language of words and Lizard's language of movement meet as one understanding now. Rippling in two hearts, one heart is felt. The answer satisfies, pulling me into the earth where I bow into this awe and fullness, which takes me into full love. I look into Ray's eyes where the same language speaks in yet another way. Reverence pulls us into silence, the language of love. Should I speak Japanese, English, or Sanskrit, Lizard comprehends, communicating clearly.

Language is a beautiful tool for expression. As a therapist who works with people of many backgrounds, I do my best to choose language that will reach the person who sits before me. While one person lights up at the use of poetry and metaphor, another feels more at home with practical facts.

When I teach graduate students, I speak a language of cause-and-effect maps. When I speak to attorneys, I speak a language based upon the question "what was heard or observed?" When I talk to philosophy lovers, I enjoy the journey of pondering without drawing final conclusions.

I adore speaking to the "senile" and "schizophrenic" because their metaphors make ABSOLUTE sense to me. They are poetic beings who express the human condition!

Language and clothes are the same. The costumes are for play, fun, beauty, art, and connecting. Because our true core is love, we can switch clothes and words while vibrating the same essential message of our being. Lizard's message is loudly transparent. "We are here together, communicating via the heart, where two different languages meet in one understanding."

Yellow Jackets Invite Vibrational Change

At Hidden Valley Sanctuary, our home, Ray, Jessie, and I share the porch with an extended family of yellow-jacket beings. This tribe is full of music and light. They come to dance on my arm and hand regularly. Never a sting. One day I forget the purpose of life. I am marching up the hill angrily and disconnected. The yellow jacket stings this one time alone.

By raising my vibration to MATCH the little yellow jacket's sting, the experience turns into a pleasurable wake-up call. As fleeting sensations move through my hand quickly, the body is alerted to vibrate faster, taking in more light. I am not a masochist and I do not like pain. However, when I raise my vibration anywhere in my body to match whatever is happening, everything becomes FULL pleasure, which passes quickly in the mist of what holds this: a deepening expanding peace. What the mind has been conditioned to conceptualize as avoided pain is in fact resistance to a vibration. I am not living in this reality steadily. I enter. I forget. I remember. I deepen. Grace takes me here. I forget again. The cycle continues. More and more, the remembering takes precedence. Yellow Jacket helps me to re-discover. Pleasure equals presence plus gratitude while matching the environment vibrationally. This pleasure comes and goes immediately, absorbed by a vast consciousness that makes no distinction in terms of more or less worthy.

As I ponder this, I squat down to pet Jessie Justin Joy. Jessie reaches his paw to my lips to be kissed. "You are a Prince," I tell him, "so your paws must be kissed." In this moment, deep happiness fills my cells, vibrating freshly with new sensations created from the bee encounter.

As this tingling love rejoices through my being, I melt into the love that holds us.

"Yes, Mother, I am here to receive your love."

"And I yours, sweet Jessie." What a beautiful planet this is. Jessie and I head back down the hill, walking in Divine Mother's morning embrace. We know now that I am forever cradled in the arms of the Divine Ma. Jessie half-closes his eyes with a soft-eye cat smile. I half-close my eyes affirming the peace between us.

Trust Yourself, Humanity, say Hummingbird Joyaya and Jonah Dove

"Trust humanity to play their parts and they will," my own heart says. Joyaya, a hummingbird who is a dear friend of mine vibrates in front of me. Two hearts share one trust.

I look up to the sky. I hear this. "You are in a theatre. It is dark. Chilly air surrounds and now the curtains are opened. The windows are open. The sun is out and filling the room. Find your dream and make it
true. Each second is born anew. Fly, winged one. You are called home. Fly. All the mystery shall be known.

Know thyself first. It has been a long time coming home. Now you are here. The rain will come in the right time. Call it when you know it is needed. It lives right here under your chin. I am but a cloud and I am also your heart."

Joyaya, cloud, and Laurie speak as one voice.

Joyaya flies toward me, way up high to the neighbor's second-floor porch, where she drinks from a flower. Morning is in a state of expectation yet simultaneously complete.

"We don't always know the fruits of our labor, why we are here, and why we do what we do. What we know most is what we love, so be who you are and all else will unfold. There are no more authorities. The teacher is yourself. Love each other and make room for the rain," I hear the clouds speak, my chest sing, and Joyaya vibrate, in unison.

"What do you hear, Joyaya?" I ask.

"Trust the rain when it comes and know when it is coming," she responds. "Though it is sunny I am instantly surrounded by cool ocean air. Feeling the cool moisture on the warm day is luxurious." Adds my little friend, "Joy!"

"Fear not the wishes of world's luring. The world beckons you with ideas that your life is lacking. You are in need. Come get this. You need that. Is that a true call? Be yourself, sweet girl, and you will rest in the Divine Mother's ever-expanding lap where the earth, the stars, and the sky sing scrumptious lullabies as one. Find your path home in your own way, taking time to meet everyone with whom you resonate here. We are all coming home. No one is wrong and everyone is right. Learn to speak your native tongue—the mother language—and rain shall come on a day when it is needed." The bottled-water delivery has been weeks late. I see the truck drive down the hill as I hear this voice. Life is curious.

"Is there anything else I need to comprehend?" I ask life.

"Be, sit, hear, know you are alive in many worlds and places which have known you before. So sit, feel, hear, see, and simply be in this familiarity."

Joyaya approaches but does not come as near as usual. Nor does she stop. She flies way up high where she rests on the upper leaves of an oak tree family member.

I ask her with my heart if she has something to share.

"I've come back, tiny me, back to the world. Come take my hand and fly!" She flies higher, circling above. "Keep coming. Don't keep going. Keep coming to me!"

I feel nourished even though the day has captivated me in love for hours such that I have forgotten to eat. Already it is midafternoon. I am full of energy, existing in other worlds, realms, and in the sun's saturating of me all at once, receiving all the nourishment I need.

"Don't go to the words. Go to your source first. Steep in light's giving. Grow with the people. Don't make them your source. Learn to live happily side by side. Each has a unique gift and expresses the same message: LOVE!"

Life showers as union. Day embraces air. Air hugs birds. Birds chirp, singing through this heart. Life is in fulfillment as herself.

I head inside and go upstairs to sit in silence. Dove Jonah appears in spirit, inviting me into a new realm. I see his beautiful white body. His face is looking around. He takes me with full trust that I will follow. He brings me to a place inside himself and inside myself. We are inside the self of everyone. In the clear air of this place there is only what is right. This place is wordless and timeless, but I have transcribed it into words as best I can.

"You need not ever again blame anyone for anything nor be disappointed in anything, for all is right. When you have blamed others and been disappointed in their responses it is because you secretly feared that you were wrong and you were at fault. In sum, you thought something about you was wrong. Nothing about you or anyone is or shall ever be fundamentally wrong. You exist in the second. There is no fault to find.

"If someone treats you unkindly, brush it away gently like a fly from your face. Whatever anyone says or does including an authority figure—not just political figures but people who profess to be perfectly spiritual and beyond others—you just accept that that is who they feel they are in this moment. They need your compassion for their imperfect human existence. You need your compassion for your imperfect human existence. What anyone does or is shall be of little concern. What is of interest to you is how you choose to respond to life in each second. The previous second is already past and not worth reviewing. Forgive whatever occurred. Ask forgiveness for your involvement. Each now is the doorway to complete devotion, love, joy, and trust. Have faith in your creator—the now: you."

Golden liquid pours through the top of my head to my throat to my heart chakra to my solar plexus to my sacral chakra to my root chakra. I am mesmerized, orgasmically alive, fulfilled, and expectant all at once. I am the lover and beloved all within my own body and my own consciousness. I am a part of consciousness that belongs to all.

Late that night Ray and I go out to eat. I see how truly sweet each person's face is. I notice it up close in the cashier who smiles, wearing an orange shirt with a slogan, "I'm a pumpkin pie." I translate that to "It's okay to love me!" How courageous he is to wear that.

The deep love I have toward many species I now have toward my species, people. Whatever realities have caused humanity to fear each other, distrust each other, violate each other's trust are being forgiven. I feel like a gift is giving itself through me. I become the embodiment of that gift as I receive it.

While I am showering that evening, many people fly through my heart. For each one love is felt. People who I appreciated people who loved me, people whose responses ruptured my heart, people who felt ruptured by me—all pass through. For them is love. It is all okay now. In love with everyone again, I melt into this.

I remembered having these feelings as a young adult, and I recalled how situations and disillusionments had chipped them away until I had these feelings only toward the animals and beings from other dimensions. Now these feelings flood me with no great expectations attached. The love simply is.

"What if I forget?" I ask Jonah.

Jonah shows me a picture of a little bird sinking to the bottom of the cage. I know that will be me if I forget. "Please choose to remember," he remarks. "Here I am. If you forget, come with me. It's easy." He trusts in me so I trust myself.

Joyaya visits Jessie and I the next morning, vibrating in front of my face, while we sit on the hill in delight. Uplifting assistance arrives continuously.

Canine: Sun's Friend

I sit on the second-floor deck of our home, perched up high among the birds and oak branches. Here I ponder how our sun stays on her post day after day, well past
the elderly years of a human's life span. She does not get the weekend off. She cannot leave work for an afternoon to go for a hike or some exercise at the gym. She doesn't
travel to a new location for some variation and a vacation. She cannot sip lemonade and recline to watch
the sunset. Her yoga is her presence in every moment—her life, her prayer. Her mediation all she is. Service is her way of life: generating to many each moment.

My most pressing question is: how is she able to feel loved and included? She's always on call, constantly in service, and forever in need by everyone. She cannot go to a friend's house for dinner to have a little private sacred time. She doesn't make love with a mate, or play a sport as a member of a team. Is she lonely? She is the elder of all friends, all unions, all teams. All this is alive in her, I find as I merge into her consciousness where she is well and full, generating and shifting with us all.

Ray understands my ongoing focus on the sun. I've been repeating my intrigue with these questions frequently. "This matter is of great interest to you," he affirms lovingly. My thoughts take me into what I become now, waves slipping into the sun's kindness, nestled in warmth. The creek sings and glimmers with laughing bells of glee below.

Early in the mornings, Jessie Justin Joy converses with the squirrels through the window. He makes a little chatter sound by clicking his jaw the way they do. When he first moved into his new body, Jesse Justin Joy had a skinny tail with long hair dangling off it. Now it has grown full and fluffy like a squirrel's tail. JJJ holds his tail up with great pride and dignity. I wonder what it feels like to carry a tail, an extension of the spine.

There is a key to feeling loved and included in all situations, which Jessie, like the sun, knows. Jessie can be part of a human family and also talk to squirrels. One day a kitten from next door invites herself into the house, where she aims to attack Jessie. She hollers. She screeches. She battles him. She is a third his size. Calmly and compassionately, Jessie stays with her, showing only kindness. He looks at her lovingly and patiently, trusting that this love shall calm her turmoil. The kitten relaxes into love's warmth, releasing some of the fear.

Ray is astounded. He takes to calling Jessie a Buddha. Clients frequently tell me that they hear Jessie speaking to them, lovingly guiding them, even though they are not used to hearing animals speak. My assistant Ken calls Jessie "Baba." Jessie is the cutest Baba I have ever met.

The sun's solo post implies a loneliness that I feel slightly, underneath layers of fulfillment, above a deeper surrender. Among many, among those I love, among those who love me back, I feel at times alone in my tasks.

"I am through with exclusion," I say. "Someone who knows the way of inclusion help me now. I am here and I am ready!"

In many days following, the canines begin to show up.

I spend many hours in a meditation spot on the back deck, created to honor all animal species. "I invite all animals with the highest intentions and deepest loving hearts to be my guides."

They come forward in a long line over a period of a year. The canines show up frequently. Some appear on the porch. Some follow me home from walks. I start closing the sliding door with just a tiny bit of room for Jessie to squeeze in because several canines show up in the house.

The canines have a secret pathway to a place in my heart that jumps, barks, and plays in delight despite anything my mind chatters. The dogs know the place where they and I are the same!

One day I am on the phone when I feel a muscular, short-haired, big body pressing against my back. I jump. It's not my soft fluff-ball feline. JJJ is an eleven-pounder and this feels like a huge body! I turn around to find a brown Lab and retriever mix about my size looking lovingly at me. "I'm home for a visit, sis," he says with alacrity.

JJJ learns a magic siddha's trick during one of the canines' visits. To avoid the dog, he jumps six feet from a lower deck to a higher one. He almost reaches the deck but begins to fall, because the jump cannot propel him the entire six feet. Somehow he maneuvers his body in mid-air to head upward another foot. There he grabs the deck, where he does a chin-up to hoist himself through the wooden railing. JJJ does this several times a day now, quite gleefully, and prefers an audience. The dog is the catalyst for JJJ's new-found fun. The dog has propelled JJJ to learn a trick that can save him should a coyote show up. The dog, in an indirect way, has brought protection.

I escort that dog home, directly to an address on his collar. He returns. We repeat this two more times. I am laughing as the events of this day fill me with satisfying humor, nourishing me to the core.

A month later, I hold a seminar at our house where someone brings another kind canine. Babel, the name on his tag, is a big, strong, and friendly charcoal-black female. Jessie Justin Joy wishes to join us in the living room but does not feel safe to come in. "This is my feline's territory," I explain. "He needs to be relaxed and comfortable to help me teach. Please take your dog outside."

"I thought that Babel was your dog," Ella says.

"No, Babel came with one of you."

It turns out that Babel had enrolled herself in the workshop, arriving when everyone else did, participating in each of the events of her own initiative. My animal-loving assistants had let her in and I had assumed she came with a person. What a bold and joyous soul!

Visits from dogs continue. On a vacation to Hawaii by myself, I go for a long hike in the woods. I come across a man miles deep into the forest. I have a very uneasy feeling that I am not fully safe. Two dogs immediately run to my sides to walk with me until the man is far behind. They escort me as though we are family.

I don't know where they suddenly came from. I call their person from their tags with my cell phone once we emerge from the trail. He is shocked that they are miles from home. The dogs themselves find nothing unusual about their travels. It is their job, they explain.

Another canine who enters my life is Troy. He is a hundred-and-forty-pound, vanilla-colored fellow. I meet him on a trail in my neighborhood. He walks with me for miles. I learn his name when we arrive back to my neighborhood road. A truck stops and the man inside says, "Is that Troy?"

"According to his collar, yes. He must be part of your family?"

"No, he's a friend of ours. We have three dogs and Troy comes over most days."

"Do you want to take him with you?"

"No, he knows his way around. He'll be over to visit us soon."

I head back home where I am met by more dogs.

Time to go back outside," I say to the household visitors, but they just roll on their backs, practically purring. One time I am taking a nap when I hear a dog collar shaking. I look up to see another canine, in the bedroom.

One of the dogs I find most endearing is Brown. Brown has hair that looks like an afro but he is not a poodle. He is bigger than a retriever. He has one brown eye and one blue. Brown enjoys bounding out of his house whenever Ray and I are walking in the neighborhood. He likes to go on walks with us, consistently running toward us and past us a few feet, looking into space nonchalantly as though he isn't the excited one. He joins us for the walk from about ten feet ahead.

He is ecstatic to have company but makes efforts to play it cool like a guy who doesn't want a woman to know how eager he is for a date. I adore Brown and am very happy when he falls in love with Blackie, a rambunctious canine who lives half a mileaway. He takes to a routine walk to the bottom of the hill every single day to see her.

Another dog who wins my heart is a big guy up the street. Before I ever meet him in person he sends me a psychic photo of himself, telling me that he shall protect me and teach me to protect myself. He is the first dog to show great sensitivity and selfless altruistic love toward me. He does not invade my house and frolic with my boundaries like some of the others. He lets me know he is there to serve and connect. I feel his fatherly presence traveling with me. This canine has my complete respect and awe.

Charcoal Beauty, a dog who lives next door to a cabin we rent in Molokai (called Molokai Paradise*), spends daily quality time with me, wherever I am. He takes me into a new realm of being. He protects me in the ocean, escorts me into heavenly energies that permeate my cells, and helps me to find ones who live in the sea. He affirms in me that dogs are heroes—selfless, mystical, patient, kind, and protecting. When I allow myself to slip into Lemurian realms, he shows up to give me instructions. When I ignore the realms of Lemuria, he runs off. He is a great teacher.

Now I encounter Cinnamon and Charles—who bring me in as family the moment I meet them at Paws and Claws Sanctuary. These two tiny dogs welcome me as though I am an old friend. I am impressed by archetypal inclusion in full gear. At the sanctuary there are more than fifty animals. All of us take a little time to get acquainted. I and most of the animal friends there need some kind of introduction and time to feel each other out. These two canines need nothing. They jump on me to kiss me as though we have known each other forever.

The map of inclusion for which I had been searching has come to me via the dogs. One day I feel sad that Troy is outside again alone, worried that he will feel excluded. However, Jessie needs to have his home territory to himself. Troy explains to me that he feels completely included. He is fully within the inclusion map, and if we were into exclusion he would go elsewhere: not in spite, not in resentment, and not in fear of exclusion but out of self-liking. Like the sun, he is a part of all he touches, he tells me. He lives in inclusion, so his footsteps naturally follow his intention and choice. Being outside doesn't separate him from us. His intention for ongoing inclusion attracts him to inclusive events and situations. "I'm part of all families wherever I am," he explains. Our hearts beat together.

Inside, outside doesn't change this. I notice it is true. My heart is beating with everyone's regardless of moods, roles, appearances, motives.

I lie on the bed compassionately, feeling the energy of exclusion that had been mine for so long. It regenerates itself into inclusion. I know in that moment that there is nothing that anyone can do to change that feeling for me. The dogs will not leave their posts. They protect inclusion, and regardless of where their bodies are and what they are doing, they are included. Inclusion is an inner state of being that they know well, as does our lovely sun onto whom I once projected loneliness.

I chose in that moment to be included, feeling the big warm sun pulsating through all of me and out of me through the bedroom window. I am included deep inside myself and everywhere as a natural extension of this choice. The dogs move with the sun in complete loyalty to this love, this breath of living in motion.

    At a party, Pepe the dachshund approaches to tell me that he needs a new door. I tell his person, Ron, about this. Ron becomes a believer in a dog's ability to communicate after not believing at all before.

    Pepe's old age has made his legs weary so that he can no longer get out of the canine door. He bumped into the door the other day. I had no way of knowing this except that I listened to Pepe. The dogs have a way of including people in the comings and goings, the needs and the cares. Pepe's extension of self moves through me to Ron, who shares this with his wife Joyce. Inclusion of moves, radiating person to person as caring warmth.

    I go outside to sit alone for a while. The sun went to sleep hours ago, but I find myself to be magically warm in the cold evening. The sun includes every being on Earth in her life. She includes herself on an ongoing basis. She does not need to change herself, her schedule, or her path in any way. Life is perfect as it is inside of her, so she easily keeps on the same path century after century for the course of her destiny. The dogs share this faith in inclusion, which is inherent, not manufactured.

I hear cricket beings as the evening falls. I appear to be alone with no other human in sight, yet I am fully included—far from any experience of aloneness, melting into the night. The canines bring me into a state of inclusion that warms the heart with embers through any kind of circumstance. Unconditional inclusion becomes my new norm. The house wall between myself and people mingling inside carries no inner boundary. As I melt into this, peace fills the refreshing night.

*www.MolokaiParadise.com

The Coyote Family

We put our new plan into action. I tell JJJ that he can go outside at 8 AM every day. Every day at 8 AM JJJ goes to the door, meows, and scratches

We put our new plan into action. I tell JJJ that he can go outside at 8 AM every day. Every day at 8 AM JJJ goes to the door, meows, and scratches the rug a bit. He never looks at the clock but his timing is impeccable. I walk around the house twice making noise with my feet, making my human presence known to our neighbors, the coyotes. I sing out a tone to make it known that we are here and warmly taking our territory.

    I do not see them, but I know they are close by. Three kills yesterday. When they kill they holler and yell and celebrate. The entire pack shares the food. The howling has been getting closer and closer to the house. After my two circles 'round our home I sing "Peace I Ask of Thee O River" into the hills where the coyote tribe lives. I don't see them, but I feel them and they feel me.

    JJJ and I stay connected all day through the heart and belly, via some magnetic force that exists far above our heads. When I call he comes cantering. When he calls I go to him. We aim to touch base with each other at least every twenty minutes. This is our family system in motion. We live moment to moment in this regard. I thank the coyotes for teaching me the value of working as a tribe in my family. Practical skill and intention are of equal importance in a third-dimensional existence.

Mama and Papa Quail are perched on a wooden plank at the top of a hill. They eye me as I watch them from behind a window. They sit alert, cocking their necks to and fro, side to side, up and down as babies and other adults in their family eat food from the ground below. Ten minutes pass and suddenly both fly up and hide behind the plank as the rest of the family disappears. Three seconds later Hawk swoops over the plank, just missing his opportunity to catch a quail. The quail family is silent.

Their tactics are well planned. Yesterday, when threatened by a potential predator, the quail family screamed together. Mama, Papa, and other species of birds took posts on the fruit trees. Loud sounding went on for half an hour. The birds know when to make sound and when to be silent for their protection. They are alert and they work as a team.

The more time I spend with JJJ outdoors, the more impressed I am. He also knows when to hide. He hears other animals long before I do. He knows when his Papa
is coming home and runs to the door long before I hear a car. JJJ knows where to position himself so that he is camouflaged to anyone in front, hidden from anyone in
in back, and safe from anyone above. He will find the right little cove at the right time, move to the top deck where nobody but the hummingbirds visit when someone
rustles in the forest, and stay in the front yard when the coyote family is near the back. He carefully places himself behind my back so that we can stay together by Joyaya's bush in the sun.

    JJJ can hear me from far away. Windows and doors closed, I can be in the house and say, "Sweet Boy!" in a soft voice that can't even be heard down the hall. JJJ turns around from far up the hill outdoors, looks straight at me, and comes running to me. When I am on the cell phone under the neighbor's outdoor stairs, suddenly a little head appears directly above. I am in the sun, sitting on the earth, and a little fur ball emerges under my legs with a little nose and two eyes looking up at me. JJJ makes life funny and fun! When I am in my office, Jessie appears on a wooden plank above the window, peering in.

It becomes increasingly clear to me that this little fellow can teach me everything I need to know about life and anything I am willing to learn. He knows the secret
Light Beings of the heavens and the earth. I feel vastly fortunate that a great teacher has chosen to live with me each day. He is far ahead of me in many ways, yet he is eternally patient with me. Whether I am half asleep or eager and alert, he is always loving, compassionate, and willing to take me as far as I am willing to go. There is no
pressure, expectation, or attachment coming from him
regarding my evolution. He offers unyielding patience, guidance when I am open, and complete trust in my ability to unfold and awaken in my own time. He is my role model.

JJJ finds delight in the most simple of things. One of his favorite indoor activities is pushing the lid off the compost bucket, finding a piece of corn on the cob, taking it out and munching. I have offered him fresh corn on the cob on a plate, but he prefers the adventure.

Watching the bathtub water spin down the drain, watching the printer expel a piece of paper, and watching the fax machine in process are of great interest. He is curious and content with whatever situation is happening in each moment. If everyone chooses to live in a state of inner peace and joy with the moment, will complex political choices be necessary or will outer peace naturally follow? JJJ doesn't discuss peace tactics. He is peace tactics and he gains my most profound respect.

It is when JJJ is next to me that I am taken into altered states and trances with other animals, elements, and spirit guides. JJJ is my channel. When Ray is near the magic deepens, grounds, and increases. We are silently bringing in the new heaven realms together, and we need each other to do so in the unique flavor we are experiencing in our home.

I am part of a big permaculture city of animals. I live nested and awakening through the grace brought to me from lizard, toad, frog, hummingbird, coyote, deer, bee, tree, and flower. My desire to make contact with Coyote grows in order to protect my feline. If your neighbors were interested in eating one of your family members, what would you do? A demonstration is of no power. A petition will go unnoticed. Who would I be fighting with these things, really? I need to be practical and take action.

    I sit on the earth and pray to my neighbors. "Please become friends with me and respect my boy's safety and my need to have him well, alive, and with me for years and years and years."

    "Come closer," I feel their call. "You are strong. Come down the hill into the woods."

    I am beckoned and something inside me says, "Go to them," while something else says, "Get a grip. You're not going down the hill to hang out with a tribe of coyotes unless you know their language inside out."

    They are not vicious murderers who kill in anger. They wish to eat like I do. "We are like your kind. Some of us are lovers of God. We treasure our family. Some of us are deeply kind.

Some of us are vastly generous. Some of us are more self-centered. There are harder workers and some who are less strong. We work together. We work in a team. We value our family. We live in a tribe. Some are here all the time and some wander off alone for a while. We are many types just like your species." The couple that speaks to me is deeply loving. I feel them with their young. I feel their love for me. My love and their love is one love. We are aware of you as we live in the forest down the hill below your house. We are your neighbors living our life as you live yours.

"Will you stay clear of my beloved JJJ? Will you let him remain here with me in safety?"

"Don't cross the line to our territory and we won't cross yours. Mutual boundaries. Have JJJ stay in his domain."

I am not quite sure what is asked of me. First I feel invited to go down the hill, but as I get closer to the coyotes in my heart I am not sure that I understand correctly. I ask my JJJ to stay close to me at all times. I announce to the locals, "I come in peace. Nobody who is in benevolence who sets foot on these lands will ever be personally hurt by me in any way. Please honor JJJ as the beloved son of Ray and me." I ask the angels and ground to help.

The next morning I wake up with the sun inside me so strong it practically pushes me down that hill. But something else restrains me. I feel I am being asked to learn something new. JJJ jumps on the bed: "Mmmmuu."

We stay together outside and JJJ looks carefully down the hill. All I can see is the forest, but he can see more and chooses for us to stay in front of the house on the other side. We move our meditation spot to a new place. I feel a male coyote with me in spirit. He is very gentle and very loving. He is warm and willing to befriend and guide me.

"You don't need to come down the hill to make peace with us. Understand that you are already down the hill in spirit. If you come in body, not everyone will understand and want to be warm and friendly. If I came to your neighborhood in body, would the people all understand and be warm and friendly? You can learn the outer ways of the coyote but you must learn in detail. That's later if you choose but not necessary for your work right now. Learn the inner ways first. Learn our ways to share with your own kind, and my wife and I will surround you with love, for we are you and you are we."

I realize that I have long misjudged this very sensitive and loving tribal animal. This is a species whose members are monogamous, who raise children as a
couple, and who share with their extended family. If anything happens to a mother, the father continues to raise his children. These coyotes that are speaking to me are beings of great love and care. They are beings of peace. I need to tune in more fully to my family member JJJ, and to my mate Ray. The coyotes are my guides. Their devotional love surrounds us, and we are all held in Divine Mother's arms.

I sit deeply cherished and protected in a bubble of coyote warmth with my JJJ. He chooses to stay close and not go on his normal morning routes. We are in a new learning phase of attunement. It is important that I learn to be aware of what JJJ is doing and where he is at all times. It is important to tune more deeply to Ray on the inner planes also.

"Can I bring food down the hill and then will you promise to keep JJJ safe?"

"Food is thoughtful, and we welcome gifts, but we make our living through the hunt. It teaches us alertness, agility, and team sportsmanship. It is our way of life. Your prayers are always answered. Know that you are here and we are here. Your wishes are honored. You are always loved."

"Is JJJ safe?"

"Yes, dear one. JJJ is always safe. Keep JJJ nearby
you, Mama Moore. Your prayers are answered.

"Is JJJ safe?"

"Yes, dear one. JJJ is always safe. Keep JJJ nearby you, Mama Moore. Your prayers are answered. Your wishes are good. We honor you and respect your ways."

I ask the other spirit guides the best way to provide protection.

"Put love first, wisdom second, and practical craftsmanship third. Dance your heart deeply in this world and the next, and all things taken shall be given on to you. We are not the way. We are simply the guides."

"What is the way?"

"To have the privilege of receiving your Master."

"Who is my Master?"

"You are. It is me, your King, who hears and speaks through you." JJJ was stretched out on the porch with his arms held out. He was relaxed as can be.

"Are you my King, JJJ?"

"I was once you and you were once me but the real King is here. He is everywhere. The Golden Palace Gates are open NOW. Your king is here! You can be home now. Go your own way and go your own style. Go together. Go alone. Go inside. Go inside. Go inside. Everyone is here."

"How?"

"There is only one way back. Love. Go now. Just go. This is your privilege, your right, and your destiny."

"Thank you."

"No, the tides have turned. I took your praise for many centuries. It is now you to whom I turn and thank. We're in partnership now."

I close my eyes and see a beautiful shape of magenta and rainbow colors pulsating and filling me up in every way I can think of. I drink and I am so full.

"I am your Father and your Father lives in you, me," a male voice says. Is he a coyote or a bird? Now I can feel both.

"Keep listening, dear." It is a kind woman's voice who now speaks. Is she a coyote or a bird? I cannot tell. All lovers and beloveds become one voice. "Keep listening, dear. The journey is no longer a lap of running and racing away. The end is here and it lives now in the beginning."

Circling our property for a walk, I encounter a magenta flower, now understanding who contacted me. The coyotes teach me to be firmly in the earth: They advise that I make my home in the beautiful chest of the muscular earth where the flowers wash consciousness with cleansing love. I feel myself rising to the ethers, an old and long-term habit. Shera, a wise Siamese cat who is with Gina as one—Shera is Sno's mentor and a dear teacher to me—often shows up in spirit when I have something to learn. She arrives, pulling me gently into my ankles and legs. Everyone is helping. I wonder where little Joyaya is. Her tiny body and sweet beak are alive in me. The love is rising in me, building, taking me somewhere new while I remain physically in the same location. I look up, grasped by the knowingness that everything and everyone, all the love, is here right now. The knowingness knows through me, embracing me in loving arms. My mind cannot hold on to this. My soul feels the perfectly clear creek water passing through me and quenching lifetimes of thirst. "This is our secret," whispers the generous coyote family. "Now it is yours too."

How the Flowers Assist

I am in the airport in Los Angeles. It is an unexpected trip. An author has called me to speak about his book on the air. I have not spent time in Los Angeles before.

What I expect is phony people plastered with make-up, hours spent getting dressed each morning, and plastic humanless faces. What I encounter are friendly, bubbly, creative people everywhere. The cab drivers and the waitresses are vibrant and talented. I am at home in this playful land. I toss my preconceived prejudice out of the cab into open air. I sing out, which is apparently fully normal here. Yeah!!!!! I am bubbly, dancing about, and at home.

I notice that a huge angel surrounds the city. She holds everyone in her arms. She is an angel of great joy and love. She loves the beings in this unique city unconditionally, holding them forever on her lap. Her image appears as a giant in the sky. She's having a grand old time!

I see that all of us are dreaming up life, each in our own movie, certain that life is the way we perceive. Some are dreaming that life is richly peaceful and others that life is challenging. I am doing a bit of both and finding the humor in this.

Later in the day I stand in line at a restaurant. The woman behind me listens over the cell phone to the ins and outs of her friend's troubled relationship with an employer. At a table to my right, someone exuberantly expresses the love she has for her husband. Someone reads the stock market pages at the bar. Someone kisses his wife. Someone spills her coffee. A toddler sings a song loudly while her mother looks at her fondly and her big sister turns bright red. There we are, all in one huge room, all together but each having a personal dream while the angel holds every single one of us in great love.

The angel is eternally patient. For those who remember the love, she rejoices. For those who forget, she loves just as deeply. She has perfect faith that
someday all people will remember how loved we are. May I remain in this love and this awareness forever?

Back home months later, I am frenzied. I vaguely remember what I experienced with the angel in L.A. "Who can help?" I call out while I lie amidst the grass and wildflowers.

White flowers come to help. They fill my eyes. They give peace.

"Should I meditate on white flowers every day?" I ask them.

"No. Let us come to you. You just needed an adjustment. You're all set."

It is true. I stand up to go for a walk around Hidden Valley Sanctuary. Now I spot the white ones who contacted me a moment ago, freshly bloomed this morning

Another day, stressed from work, I lie on the porch. Soon my eyes are dazzled by an intricate yellow design that fills me with glee, reverence, and excitement. It looks like a beautiful painting. Now I understand how visual artists get their ideas—they come to them. An angel tells me that she has come and that she lives in a daffodil.

A few days later I find a yellow daffodil that has grown unexpectedly by the side of our house. We recognize each other as familiar.

Often I watch my clients and notice that they are lost in dreams they are making up, psychological troubles that truly don't exist, and manufacturing realities that the age of psychology has conditioned them to believe in. I spent years in these places myself and am not at all beyond reentering them. I ask some red flowers that grow in a pot on our porch about this. "What do I do?"

"You are strong. Use your wisdom. Give them alternative ways of looking at things and they too will create miracles. It's their birthright. As your clients create new perceptions, as they enter into the miraculous zone, their discoveries are magnified in your own heart. They live in your heart as you live in theirs. The flowers are solid in their faith, still in their strength, and full with the life of water. I became braver about offering entirely different perspectives to clients, and clients became happier.

A recent study states that happy couples in my age range have sex sixteen times a month. "Maybe I should keep track. I don't know how many times we have sex in a month," I say laughing about these kinds of studies. Humans like to measure things and I find humor in this.

But the reply is serious. "You are always having sex ... all day," a purple flower tells me. It is true. I am surrounded by flowers, sexually fulfilled each moment in
the waves of existence. My heart and womb are orgasming by just existing.

"I'm tired," I complain. "Maybe I need some supplements."

"Drink water!" I hear. "It works wonders." Green leaves spoke. They were right. Three big glasses and I am abundant with energy.

I decide to work out more often. "I wish to get stronger," I call out. "What is the best method?"

"Do your work in whatever way you are called to do so moment by monet. Share stories. Offer silence. Give care. Write of your experiences. Live!" sing out the geraniums, quivering with wonder in the breeze. When I follow the guidance, I become stronger.

"I still need more help to complete my books!" I exclaim. The peas flash a picture. There are so many of us that we are rich with each other. Water is delivered to us from the sky! All we need is here. Abundance overflows. Help is always here.

Friends call to say that they going important places. Maybe I should go too. I can feel that they are called and I feel they are happy. "Should I go to an energy center?" I ask the ground. "Maybe I need to help out in other places."

"This is an energy center. You are here and you are home." It is true. Everything I need is inside.

I say, "Dear Divine Ma, please fill me with satisfaction and let me release all thoughts of lack."

Lizards scamper in the bush. Dragonflies pass by. Together we know the fullness of each breath.

Who Is Calling Whom?

Looking into the water, at Elkhorn Slough, on a day-long kayak trip with Ray, memories filter through this heart. Sun filters through the day. Recognition blooms in the air along with sun warmth. The animals have been calling to me all along. I have been calling to them. A great Love generates from our union.

. Many joyful memories pass through my heart's consciousness.

When I was five, Mom took me across the street to meet the kittens. "They were recently born and have never left their mother," our neighbors explained. "Don't touch them."

We arrived. I did as I was asked. A little silver tabby girl called "Tiger" walked right to me. It was her first time away from her mother. Everyone was surprised but me. We became best friends, spending wonderful time together every day until I left for college. Even then my sister, Tiger, was with me in spirit.

Each morning, Mom would get up earlier than I, and when it was time for me to get up to go to school she would say, "Tiger, go get Laurie." Tiger would dash down the hall, jump on my bed, and rub my face with hers over and over, cuddling me and purring.

When I was seven I learned to ride horses with a saddle. One time the teacher said I could try bareback. I eagerly got on the horse's back, not understanding that if I got on her lower back it would cause her discomfort and she would buck me off. I landed on my head. The immediate concussion came and went in an instant so I remember none of it other than what my father told me years later. I do know that after that experience, I was very afraid of horses and decided to quit the lessons, even though I didn't completely understand why.

It was Tippy Sue who encouraged me to love horses again. She was one of the biggest and strongest horses at summer camp. She was white with gray spots. When I went to pet her she motioned to move that head through the reins for me. She comforted me and gently assured me that she would never hurt me. I was safe. It was okay to calm down and relax. She was like a parent to me.

Throughout my childhood animals would show up at our house. They knew where to come. A grey curly poodle named Blackie got hit by a car many houses away and was in great need of immediate veterinary care. She made the arduous journey in an extremely painful condition, arriving in our carport. We took her to the vet.

Numerous cats came. Some came in need of medical help and others moved in.

One year in elementary school I received a science kit as a birthday present. I took my small jar, full of breathing holes, and began to collect caterpillars. It became a game. The more I had, the richer I felt. Soon the jar was so full that the caterpillars were crawling all over each other. I decided to let them out and found that one had begun to build a cocoon. Surrounded by a practically impossible situation, no space, only some water drops to drink but no food, that little caterpillar was so determined that she was building a cocoon. My heart broke. I realized that we are of the same spirit though living in different bodies, and I vowed to never collect or mistreat bugs again.

As a teenager I was a camp counselor. I loved to make the kids laugh. My friend PJ was a sweet cat who was deaf. I was joking around and told people that I was
speaking sign language to him. "Come visit me in my cabin in ten minutes," I pretended to say with my hands. PJ watched intently.

There were fifteen cabins and numerous other buildings on the camp property. Ten minutes later there was a knock at my cabin. I went to the door. It was PJ. He came in and jumped up to one of the top bunk beds: mine!

Cats let me know that they are very astute. In England, where I attended a year of graduate school, I missed being around animals. I wished a cat would visit me one day. That evening, a cat seemed to appear from nowhere, in my bedroom. She came in for some cuddle time and left.

I decided it was time to live with a cat again, years after Tiger had passed on and I was a young adult. As soon as I decided that, cats appeared everywhere. I walked out of the grocery store and found that a gray and white one had jumped into my car when I left the window open. As I put her outside she looked at me surprised, as if to say, "Weren't you the one who called?" I visited friends and cats ran to my lap. I walked down the street and a Siamese cat appeared at my feet.

"I'm going to share this home with a cat," I told a friend.

"What kind?" she asked.

I hadn't thought about it but as soon as she asked a big orange cat flashed into my mind. "A big orange one."

The next day, the stray neighborhood cat who was big and orange moved himself in. I was dating a man not of my dreams at the time, who was out of town. Two weeks later when he arrived he said, "I can't believe you are letting a cat inside. He will pee on everything." I was mortified that he would say such a thing in front of my well-behaved feline friend, Bhakti Santi Pop Jones, the big orange feline.

Bhakti did not ever pee on anything of mine, but on that day only, he left his poop right in the middle of that boyfriend's pile of clothes. Soon I realized it was time to end the relationship with the boyfriend and felt much happier!

Turned out that Bhakti had several homes and several names. He was a guest who spent a lot of time with me. He had a great sense of humor and brought me great fulfillment for our short time together.

A few years before I issued my invitation to the animals to connect with me, I was swimming in the ocean by myself. I did a double-take and realized that a man with a big mustache had approached and was staring at me. He was bald. I looked again. He was a sea otter!

Ray and I continue kayaking at Elkhorn Slough. The afternoon is full of silent ease. A little sea otter jumps into my lap. The animals are our friends. They are our sisters and brothers.

Wings and Trunks of Support

My partner, my feline companion, and I share land with a group of quail and several bay trees, among many other animals and plants. One of the bay trees, who lives outside my front window, is a singer. When I am very quiet deep inside myself I can hear her sing a song of eternity. She sings in love that has no beginning, no end, and exists in a realm of all time. She sings an endless tone. I call her Liaya (pronounced Li-ay-ya).

Her dear friend, Brandon Delicious, another bay tree who lives in the back yard, often keeps company with Jessie and I. Sometimes I sleep outside, right underneath Brandon. This tree often offers me advice on how to ground my dreams in the real world. He tells me to bring all stories of goodness I write to the earth. "Plant them there, by sitting on the ground and imagining these stories taking root," encourages Brandon Delicious. "This way they will bloom again for others to hear, many years from now, after your Laurie body is gone."

Brandon Delicious sends visual images to me. He shows me that he has not always had enough water but he has remained healthy. He plans to stay intact when times are turbulent. He tells me I must sink my own roots deep if I too wish to stay intact.

Quail who live on the land with us are admirable neighbors who value family. Recently a flock of babies was born, and I have watched them crossing the driveway with their parents. Mom accompanies while Dad follows to protect. When I think an inspired thought from my heart and soul such as "Love is my only true purpose," or "I open myself to hearing the guidance of my spiritual mentors, the animals," the quail tribe makes a clapping sound.

The clap sound is actually one of their forms of protection. It startles predators away. However, the natural world will forever mirror itself. If I am in a state of reverence and someone in the natural world is in a state of reverence, we will find each other. We synchronize without trying. We speak of different meanings that become part of one event. We find new messages in each other's practices. We respond to each other in a dance of grace, a language of the universe, that is simple to understand and overflowing with love.

Often when I wake up in the morning, my ego is temporarily gone like a pair of dark glasses that fell off my face. I forget the glasses for a while. Then I pick them up from the floor. Soon a thought of judgment invites my ego back, but prior to that I am in a fluid world. During this open morning time, I find myself flown into the sky—judgments, burdens, and goals all lifted from me as this soul dissipates into the trees surrounding. It is the hawks who soar above my home, fly over my car, and circle above places I visit, helping me. Ever since I prayed to the animals to teach me their wisdom and their ways, the hawks have been friends. They have the wisdom to take me to realms I did not discover through the human maps.

    Joyaya shows up when I am feeling delighted and joyous. When I am outdoors she approaches me at face level and looks toward my eyes while remaining in flight and humming with her sweet fast-beating wings. Sometimes she zooms in and hovers above me or presents herself in a circular dance. When I am inside she will find me also. She can locate the window I am nearest to and come close to that window.

    Sometimes when I am in the kitchen chopping vegetables and I begin to contemplate the human psyche, the people around me, and other complex matters, Jonah reminds me to listen more deeply to my heart, where I can feel him. Here it is clear and there is no need to figure anything out, for love is all I need to know.

After being a designer and leader of classes, seminars, troupes, productions, and events for thirty-four years (I started when I was seven), I feel a need for a new role. I loved being a leader but now I am ready to be a collaborator. I ask for animal guidance and hear back from elephants, swans, and herons long-distance. One night as I am slipping into sleep I am jolted telepathically by elephants: "Wake up!"

    I laugh first, then alertly sit up to listen. They show me what it is like to be an elephant. To stomp massive legs and feel the vibration of communication moving through the legs is a powerful and grounding experience. To swoop a trunk into the air and feel the chakras of the throat, face, and trunk tingle with ecstasy that vibrates out into the tribe is an event of incarnated physical bliss.

    The elephants tell me that they value the love among them beyond the individual's mission. They tell me that in valuing this love each individual is taken in with profound regard, respect, and wonder. "Solve the troubles of the individuals in your culture by valuing Love first.

Then your individuality will be a celebratory event in motion instead of a competitive weapon."

White birds approach, informing me that they have a similar experience of family as the elephants, although to feel like one of them is very different. "To pierce through the wind in a straight line with great trust in the bird who is in the lead and complete connection to all the birds flying in the flock is the greatest joy of ours. We trust our leader because our leader is us. In your human world you question authority because authority can operate in individual interest and require questioning. In our flock, the one in the lead is one with us, and we delight in the journey as one. There is no better/worse hierarchy when we are in flight. We simply are."

After visits from these animals I call together a gratitude circle for the human species, asking that we all lead. In this, each person's gifts become clearer and stronger to me. I can be a leader by being part of everyone, in a way that follows their hearts. This intrigues me, allowing me to rest yet play at the same time.

The birds, the trees, the elephants, and the many members of the natural world are forever willing to take our hands and help us. Dove Jonah tells me that he will stay with me forever, even beyond body. I trust him with all my heart and soul. He will forever guide me back to love because his intention and choice is to exist as pure goodness and grace.

One day I work diligently to invoke love in my office no matter what good or bad news, joy or sorrow, positive or negative attitude is brought in. I stay focused on being love throughout it all, having a day full of tingling joy and curiosity. As the day ends, however, I find myself tired. Jolliness wanes. I am left feeling depleted. "I need a hand," my heart calls out.

I stop by a grocery store on the way home. While driving into the parking lot, deeper weariness saturates me and I begin to feel ill at ease. "Please, carry me, great Spirit," my soul sings.

"I can't do this alone," I think to myself. Out of nowhere and everywhere two mallards head toward my car's front window. The experience feels like a modern-day fairy tale. In the middle of the city, just off Main Street full of traffic, in a parking lot for a grocery store, one female and one male mallard arrive. They approach

quickly. When about a foot away, they gracefully swoop and arc up above me. At that moment I feel them pass my burdens to the sky to evaporate. I know that I am forever carried and held by the kindest wings and the strongest legs of support on planet Earth when I listen to my teachers. "I am you and you are me."

Coming Home

A gorgeous white butterfly passes by. On a day of many unusual clouds that look like modern dancers jumping into the sky, I hear the words, "You are home. Now you are home." I feel as though I am a swan in flight with big trustworthy wings. I realize where I am and that I have been in a daze for four decades, perhaps many lifetimes. But the daze is now gone, so there is not much to say about it.

Now is the Garden of Paradise. Without moving, I have entered a new place. Everything smells kind. Jessie Justin Joy is by my side. Each bird that flies by sounds sweet.

"You ask and you receive," I hear. "You've pruned your vines each day so the grapes are abundant for you. They always were and now you find them. The great mystery is answered and the great mystery continues. The grapes are forever yours."

I have been lost in a spell for as long as I can remember. A recent disappointment with a choir, Jessie Justin Joy's daily insistence that I spend more time outdoors, and Shera's recent answer to my question "How do I stop being angry?" now catapult me into Heaven while I remain here on Earth. The braided strands of frustration, longing, and misery became so intense that I asked for something new. Heaven is the answer—allowing my heart to fill up with Heaven as the animals have encouraged me to do repeatedly.

Two weeks earlier, Ray and I were approached by a thoughtful green grasshopper who took time to say hello and share some warmth. It is said that the grasshopper symbolizes a big jump. When one comes to you, expect to take a huge leap of growth. The time is now. The gift is here.

I have secretly used much of the past twelve months to create a surprise fiftieth-birthday ritual for Ray. The music is being arranged and conducted by a favorite musical group in town. They committed to taking charge of this aspect of the party and ritual almost a year ago, keeping me thinking that they were practicing and getting it ready. But four days before the event, without a previous warning clue, they suddenly back out.

I spend much of the next twelve hours emailing and calling every local musician and dancer friend I can think of. I am calling for a group to create the grand entrance event from scratch with one rehearsal. In less than a day, blessing brings a new group of seven to replace the old: dancers, a bell ringer, singers, and guitarists. I rearrange numerous plans and people who are involved in helping, so we can create the new welcoming plan. I arrange for Ray to be detained so I can conduct preparation rituals with the musicians and the eighty guests.

With the hew plan quickly put into motion, I have two hours to rejuvenate. With my back is on the yoga mat and my legs are in the air, I slow down. Leaving the quick energy of reorganization, relaxed into emotions, I feel waves of irate energy move through me. I am unable to forgive the group who broke their promise on such short notice, even though I wish to forgive, even though things are working out anyway. The betrayal hits a deep chord. The harder I try to release my anger, the more it takes hold of me. I contact Shera the feline to ask her what to do.

Shera doesn't seem to understand my question. "What are you doing now?" she asks.

"I'm coming up with a new musical event, thinking of songs, and getting ready to lead a rehearsal. I'm exercising my body and feeling a lot of energy in my chest."

Shera notes that I am abundant with people, rich with creativity, blessed with music, and exercising my body happily, while emotions pass through. To her, whatever the musicians did or didn't do yesterday isn't happening. That has nothing to do with anything. She seems puzzled by me. "Only now is here," she expresses.

Her understanding fills my heart. I begin to feel exhilarated with now, with the musicians who are coming, and mostly with my stepping back into an old role, now with a collaboration aspect. In my twenties I was the leader of many performances, rituals, and rites of passage and I loved it. An opportunity is here! The surge in my chest expands into elation. Joya, a guitarist, vocalist, songwriter, and friend I performed with fourteen years ago, calls to say she is coming. She cackles about it all. "This is Divine Disorder at its best, so expect blessings!" She will bring a new CD she recently produced along with an original song. She and I will be at the doorway to sing together when Ray enters. This seems a lot more enjoyable than the original plan!

The blessings are here! I am catapulted into the joy of now in the wealth of who I get to be: me. I know exactly what to do in the face of unexpected change and am doing it. I begin to celebrate with all my heart. What a blessing! A gift has come in an odd package.

On the day of the party Jessie Justin Joy and I do our morning meditation by some shrubbery. Usually I start the day on the porch where Joyaya the hummingbird comes to see me, but we decide to be hidden today, tucked between the garden fence and some bushes. Joyaya reminds me that she can find me anywhere. She flies up to me, only a few inches from my face, then perches herself on a tiny branch a foot away, looking at me closely. Her body weighs about an ounce. What a sweet soft little being! Jessie Justin Joy remains relaxed. I thank him for choosing Joyaya as a friend. He purrs and bathes himself.

As Joyaya and I look at each other for a long time, Jessie sitting peacefully with his little head resting on my leg, I am melted into the richest joy I have ever found. I turn into my heart. All that exists is love. Earth nourishes and feeds me as I lay my back on her, becoming fuller, whole, and complete than I have ever been before.

I realize that my job is to create a ritual that will invite everyone into this space of endless ecstasy. I lie for hours unable to speak, burning up with indescribable, incomprehensible love. Being the lover of life has been easy for me. Now I become the beloved. The air, the trees, Joyaya, Jessie, the earth, and many spirit guides infuse me with endless love. Everything is love. I am cradled, held, showered, and fed with love. Each time I feel full, more is given to me and I became fuller, with more to give.

When the guests arrive I share the story of Joyaya, asking everyone to choose one quality they most appreciate about Ray. "Hold that quality in your heart. Think about ways you have seen Ray demonstrates this quality. Now think about ways you have experienced this quality yourself. This event is to honor Ray, and in honoring Ray we honor ourselves. We honor our species: humanity." The energy is rising, so when Ray arrives he notes that the house energy has been fully transformed.

Tanya dances plays her drum, perched on a large and strong tree branch. Richard, who already passed the threshold of fifty, takes Ray over the line to his new world. Richard shares the blessings of this time period with Ray. The fifties is a time to discover your most authentic self, he expresses. A group of us sing as Ray walks in. One by one, each friend comes up the stairs to greet him with great love. Ray is crying deeply with gratitude. People are in a state of joy.

Jessie Justin Joy stays in the bedroom for some quiet, holding the space of love for all with male feline energy. In his eleven-pound body lives a proud lion who holds himself with great grace and male strength. He receives human visitors, while little fairy beings dance around him. It is becoming increasingly evident to me that nothing is as it appears. The only way to know what is happening is to listen to my heart. What looks strong is often weak, and what looks meek may be made of the strongest substance the Earth has to offer.

When we hold sacred circle later in the night Jessie comes out, greeting most of the people in the circle one by one. Jessie sits on Ray's lap as the meditation begins. The more I trust my heart and the less I trust the ways in which I have been educated, the happier I become. Life is feeling like a magical fairy tale in which the gates to Heaven have been opened. We all can feel like wealthy queens and kings among the abundant greenery.

A couple of days later I sit in a chair on the back deck, suddenly feeling the energy of the choir director. He had no choice but to back out of the party plans due to his group's lack of commitment. He was willing and generously available. Now I also notice that there is a current longing, a sadness that he is addressing inside his soul. He is working through something in his life, and this was not the right time for him to have been holding the energy here. He is a great man who held the energy for many events, creating great joy for tens of thousands of people over the years. Ray's party was not the place and time for him to do so again. I understand that universal flow arranged this change. At this time forgiveness floods my heart.

No mistakes have been made and no injustice created. The universe knows best and everyone has played their contributing part. My anger becomes compassion, as I realize that leading the ritual myself was a blessing. I had spent months and months creating the event, and it was my job to carry it to completion. The Divine had knocked on my door and invited me to do what gives me the most joy.

I look to the canyon, feeling wealthy with the peace that many trees can bring. I realize that I am not who I thought. I thought that Ray, JJJ, and I were the center of this sanctuary-world, fortunate to be surrounded by other forms of life.

Now I realize that I am actually a member of an intricate eco-village comprised of many birds, reptiles, mammals, insects, and humans. All of them except the humans are master permaculturists. I am in school by living, but uneducated in the language of most of my teachers, my village mates. I do not speak anyone's native tongue. I would have to sit in the trees, walk on the grass, lie on the ground, and listen very deeply for many hours and days to learn the languages that are here.

The voices of the choir members who I thought had "abandoned me" are everywhere. Nobody has left. Everyone is home. There is a song in the air. Liaya the tree is singing her song to the sky. She has never stopped. Tape recordings of the human choir are playing in the air. I can feel the echoes of concerts I have attended. Next I hear, "Stay tuned. We are coming to greet you." I am flying and settled all at once.

The Courier Beetle Pays a Visit

Something good has become of me. I spend a lot of my time happy and giddy with being. I used to be busy finding important things to do. Now I favor watering the peas and picking them, eating and sharing the cucumbers with friends, and walking around the house while staring at my rose-painted toenails. This gives me absolute delight!

It is summertime and close to midnight. I have been meditating in the gathering room, where people attend seminars. I am about to get up and retire for the evening when I notice a frantic beetle. He is huge—about the size of my entire thumb. He is on the second floor of the house, outside on the window desperately trying to get in. Wearing a fancy design on his shell, he looks like he has just gotten home from a trip to Nieman Marcus, seeking a friend to view his new outfit. This guy's eyes are so big that he looks like a little Martian with very large ear shapes attached to his antennae.

The windows on the side of the gathering room span fifteen feet, so he could have perched himself anywhere. Somehow, he and I end up eye to eye without trying. He looks at me as he wiggles his arms, searching for a way to get through the glass. I look at him in curiosity.

What is he up to? This beetle has the entire outdoors available to him. The night is not particularly cold. He is not trapped. He can fly off the window in a second. He can climb back down to the ground. He can take a nap on the window sill. He may scuttle himself up to the roof. His options are endless, yet he insists on trying to get through the glass. What is up with this guy?

My interest in him magnifies. I wish to be closer to him. He appears to be navigating himself to be closer to me.

I tune more deeply into his humming vibration, feeling intense determination but no indication of what draws him here. I call him Ted. "Do you need something from me?" I ask. The more I feel this beetle's presence, the more I feel the tenacity of his perseverance.

"Did you come to receive something from me?" I inquire of him again. I feel a "yes" but no clarity on what it is. Moments pass. The conversation remains suspended, incomplete. Eventually I leave to brush my teeth. As I exit the gathering room, Ted bangs the window three times.

Quickly returning, mesmerized by Ted's certainty that we must connect, I relax on the couch. "Was that him before?" I ask Ray. I had heard banging about a half hour earlier and couldn't figure out who or what it was. But Ray is already dozing on the sofa, leaning on my shoulder with Jessie Justin Joy by his leg. I felt comforted by their presence and increasingly curious about Ted.

Then something dawns on me. During the morning I had received a phone call from a local restaurant. The staff was a close group who considered themselves to be somewhat like a family although nobody was blood-related. One of the members named Dave, a man who was well-liked and whose work was central to the restaurant's success, had chosen to commit suicide yesterday. I was called to arrange a gathering for the staff and would be leading it tomorrow.

"Are you here on behalf of the suicide?" I ask Ted.

At last the beetle settles down and so do I. He relaxes himself on the ledge, quiet and serene. What a beautiful divine messenger this beetle is, so loyal to his cause that he flies 25 feet to a second floor, locates me, and will not give up. He is the courier.

Together we sit in a silent meditation. Ray and Jessie have a meditative presence whether they are awake or asleep. They join us from dreamland. As I am soothed into trust and wonder, the courier delivers a message.

Dave understands that you are conducting a gathering on his behalf. He feels that you are fully focused on his survivors and not including him very much. He desires to be accurately represented.

I am happy behalf of Dave. A number of people who have passed over contact me. Often relatives of those passed call me to translate communications from their loved ones on the other side. I don't spend a lot of time differentiating anymore. Angels, devas, saints, and other masters who live in higher dimensions, people on this side or the other, animals and insects are all souls communicating essential wisdom in love.

Dave expresses that he made an error and now wishes to come back. If he had the capacity to digest the love and care that was here for him on Earth before he left, he would have stayed. Now he can fathom it, but it is too late.

"Go to the light," I communicate to this soul. "Go to the light. You are making the same mistake all over, Dave. You wanted to leave so you could get rid of your pain. Now you want to come back to get rid of your pain. You can find another body and come back but it won't work. You will keep that pain with you everywhere you go until you choose joy instead."

I know this MO. In my twenties I moved to England, moved to a commune in Virginia, and moved to Boulder pursuing a pain-free life, but every move made the emotional heart-longing pain worse. It was only when I decided to value joy above pain that the pain shrank and shrank and finally dissolved. It was when I sank fully into the pain with no resistance that it transformed its flavor.

My words seem to touch and affect Dave, who now appears by the beetle. Yet I feel Dave yearning for something a lot deeper than my advice. I sit with him, heart to heart, embracing him fully in the state he is in. I abandon any attempt to teach, change, or help him, instead simply loving him as he is right here, right now. I feel some peace in him. He squirms, making a shaking feeling in my heart, next taking in nourishment to soothe himself.

I feel that the time has come for Ray, JJJ, and I to head off to bed. We seem to have the same idea, each getting up to leave the living room. The courier beetle remains on the sill. I nod a Namaste and good night to Dave, who fades back into the realm of his current existence. Gliding into my own dream world, I realize that I too have been pushing away support that is readily available. Feeling fully nourished in the realms of animals, nature, and my family, I am very blessed. Simultaneously I have huge debt, am not finding the means to pay it back, am continuously giving hours of free labor and discounts, and simply do not trust the world to ever fully take care of me financially.

Courier Beetle Ted tells me, "The world will give you what you desire, but you must ask the world for that. You must be available to receive the gifts. You can be fine financially. Really, it's what you ask for and what you are willing to receive that reflects the love in your finances. However, you must ask in complete innocence and trust, with complete openness and no dictations on how, when, and where. No specifics. Full openness to your general desire being fulfilled is your key."

Worries dissipate as troubles evaporate. A brand-new experience of feeling completely trusting and cared for on the financial plane fills me up. My financial worries are replaced with financial ease as I float into the waves of life, drifting into color and joy, images of the day, and peace of this night.

The next morning, when I go to sit with the restaurant staff, two squirrels are making love on a driveway that I pass. Birds and dragonflies have been very bold about making love before Ray and me, which has felt quite magical and charming.

However, this seems rather public to me. "Are you certain you want to make love by a busy road?" I ask. Two little jubilant voices reply, "Be well. Be well. All is well. Nothing is wrong. Nothing is right. Bad it is not. It's not good and it's not better. No, it isn't worse. Beings are being born. Beings are eating. Beings are love-making. Beings are dying. Today some are building. Others are conversing. All is well. All is swell. Nothing is hidden. Nothing is gone. All is here."

When I greet the staff at Dave's workplace, I tell them that every sharing is welcome. "You will all have highly different experiences. Some will have unexpected spiritual discoveries. Some will feel strong emotions. You may cry. You may laugh. You may be angry at Dave for what he did. You may have full empathy for what he did. Someone will surprise himself or herself with ecstatic feelings of joy and gratitude for life. Someone will feel guilty, but it's neither your fault nor Dave's. It's simply a choice he made. You may feel very sad. Someone will feel nothing and that too is fine.

"You will feel whatever is you today. You are in flux. This event will bring you into a more intimate experience of yourself, and everything about yourself is fully welcome. All your feelings are welcome. None are right. None are wrong. None are better. None are worse. Please support and encourage each other to experience whatever you do.

"You do have one choice. You can use Dave's choice to commit suicide as inspiration, or you can use it to become discouraged. He chose to die and undoubtedly had many feelings surrounding this. I invite you, without making him wrong, to choose to live fully, always, wherever you are. Your feelings will come and go, and while they do you can focus on your despair or your gratitude. Those who focus on despair will find more and more pain. Those who focus on gratitude will find more and more joy. If you don't agree, consider it an experiment and give it a try."

Someone expressed that she felt deep empathy for Dave and was simultaneously angry at him. "I feel guilty about the anger," she said.

"That anger probably got you a lot of places. Did you get angry at yourself at a time when you wished to give up?"

"Well, yes."

"Did it keep you from giving up?"

"Yes."

"Sounds like that helped you, and if Dave were here listening, it might help him also. Could you allow yourself to feel deep empathy and anger both, and accept yourself for this paradox?"

"Yes, I can."

Dave's death has helped me through a tremendous passage. I am grateful to him, trusting that he can choose a joyful next step if he desires. That is my hope for him but not my responsibility.

When I arrive home I sit on the porch, thinking about what happened over the last twenty-four hours. Someone is calling out from a tree. He calls three times but no mate replies. I look behind me. Way up high, almost camouflaged by the oak leaves, his visage shows slightly in the sun. He is a big blue bird. I turn toward him. Then he flies back to the forest silently.

I think of Kent, the owner of the business who was the one to find his staff member no longer breathing. Kent's eyes are large and circular like Brent's. Brent is a big male deer with antlers that show him to be about three. He does not carry himself with a light dainty presence, as do most deer. He is very grounded. Often after I complete a meditation on our porch I look up and there he is in the only place I ever see him, face framed by the greenery of his favorite eating spot. When I look up he is looking at me. We look at each other.

As I think of the similarities between Deer Brent and human Kent, two kind males with a presence that welcomes and gives me a feeling of safety, I feel a tunnel at the bottom of my heart. Deep inside there is only one of us.

The Language of Love:
Cyclical, Ongoing Learning with My Ever-Present Animal Friends

We learn the same life lessons again and again, delving more deeply into their essence each time. We spiral and cycle through love that lightens, expands, and falls further into the endless each time we revolve through a familiar lesson with a loved one.

When I treat life with a willingness to cooperate, all life becomes my teacher and my lover. Recently I experienced some cramping during my menstrual flow. Believing that my ovaries have a life of their own and were expressing something to me, I decided to be my ovaries for a while. I took my consciousness and feeling awareness into my ovaries. It became apparent that some sorrow was living there.

I saw pictures of events that happened many years ago, which had lodged themselves in my ovaries. As I remained fully present, fully accepting the ovaries' experience, the pain intensified. I was one with the pain so it no longer hurt. I was placing my consciousness in the ovaries instead of analyzing them. The pain was merely a sensation. As I remained present, the pain subsided. I took the pain to my heart (a practice suggested by Margaret Ruby, who is the founder of Possibilities DNA) and forgave it. My ovaries felt a tingling joy. I was in love with life.

During a visit, Sno's person tells me that Sno has become calmer since the two of us recently spent time with one another. Sno has also repeated being stand-offish among some guests. My heart tells me again that Sno is a very loving and sensitive little being. I feel her to be playful, and she affirms that this is so. These are her thoughts sent through my heart. We feel and think together. She sends me heart-telepathic pictures of herself as an acrobatic healer, bringing me great delight and joy. When I approach her she hisses. Her outer behavior doesn't match what I feel she is communicating to me from within, so I remain curious.

I keep my focus on the love I feel she is sending to me. Later in the day when I have left her home and am alone, I send gratitude from my heart to hers. My heart tells me that this sweet white girl with Andara Avalon crystal-blue eyes is a sister and dear friend. I realize that her hiss is simply a communication that I stepped over her boundaries by coming too physically close, eager to cuddle her.

Next time I see Sno I apologize for stepping over her boundaries and say, "If you want to touch me, please reach out your paw or rub your body against mine. I will not violate your boundaries again. I will not touch you unless you show me that you wish to touch." She looks at me with eyes that say "Thank you."

Ten minutes later she rubs her body against me, reaching out for my hand with both her paws. Apparently this is unusual behavior for her, because people often leave her alone after she hisses. The love between us begins to tingle in my heart like precious bells chiming. Sno looks into my eyes for a very long time. I feel myself being freshly born into a new world.

    We can bring each other into new births repeatedly: humans and animals, animal and animals, humans and humans! In an openness to the heart's song of now, each beginning breath is a unique experience, flavored with similar themes. I call this world the palace of Divine Love. I feel myself being transported with this wondrous princess to a very clear, pure place where all is ecstatic, sweetly sacred, and intoxicatingly delightful. During the experience I am both in Heaven and on Earth at the same time. I begin to cry with gratitude and innocence recalled from childhood.

    As I reflect on the experience, I realize that this Divine master teacher has given me an important key for awakening. Cherish and protect your Divinity. My feline guide is willing to respond to me when I speak to the love in her with the love in me in the realm of mutual respect. We have been here before, and now we revisit this awareness as newborns. Each cycle is fresh, intoxicating nectar from the Divine. So as not to dilute the clear essence where she remains present, Sno needs me to adjust my energy, approaching her gently. By tenderly demanding complete respect, she transports me to a place I would not have entered otherwise.

I feel that this feline can see me at a very deep level, recognizing the angel in me as well. Each of us has an angel inside, deep within the most loving part of us. My cat friend is affirming to me in a wordless language that my individual way is my sweet gift. In flowing with what feels true to my heart I become both the receiver and offering of this Divine gift: myself. This profound feline being has invited me to bring out my purest self. In responding I become more at home in myself. I also feel profoundly seen and heard.

All beings in life have something to offer. While I continue my studies at animal

communicator Gina Palmer's sanctuary, I am blessed to spend time with
many doves. One of them, Jonah, sits on my solar plexus. I listen to him with my belly and heart. As I listen he invites me to feel fullness with him. Jonah translates the feeling of fullness to me from him. I learn that feeling full is a choice.

"If you want to be full, be full. Choose full," Jonah tells me. "It's easy!"

Since my first visit with him, any time I think a thought that is a complaint or negative, I quickly erase it with a new thought, one of fullness and joy. Jonah teaches me that nothing can fill me up. Fullness is simply a state of being to choose. If I choose partially full, I am actually placing some of my consciousness on lack, so I choose completely full. For the first time in my life, I know I can choose fullness each moment instead of filling up with outer experiences that will later dissipate.

One of my clients is feeling suicidal on the day that he arrives for his first session. He has been struggling with suicidal desires for ten years. Together we come to the conclusion that he needs to be accepted exactly as he is. Together we practice accepting everything he feels and thinks with love, assuming it is all part of life. We both notice that acceptance leads to new doors. When we accept him fully for who he is as a human, discordant parts of both him and me begin to redirect themselves back toward harmony. Through this mutual practice, both of us come to spend a lot more of our existence in states of joy, fulfillment, and love. I have come to trust that life itself knows more than me alone. I feel that life sent this client to me (and me to him) for my learning as well as his. Life knows what she is up to!

Each day I ask the wind, the earth, the sun, and the water for guidance. I feel my body transforming into a temple of ecstatic love, waking up in more and more places. Often my heart is so joyful I feel I will burst, but the Earth cradles me and shows me that moving into happier and higher vibrations is the invitation of the time. I begin to feel orgasmic in all my chakras as a natural state of being, and my body becomes able to handle deeper and deeper states of ecstasy and love. The ticket has been to choose love and respect for all life. The ongoing concert is a life in which my teacher and lover is everyone. I often feel my body as a small aspect of the huge vast love and Oneness we all are. Others say they are experiencing similar states in this era of evolution.

Last week I apologized to a plant in my house for neglecting her, and to my heart she spoke: "I celebrate our love today. Whatever happened before is of no concern to me." She demonstrates beautiful unconditional forgiveness and the magic of choosing love. She is happy and content, with no need to ponder over whatever happened in the past. Regardless of any past circumstances, she is here to be love in the moment.

I share these experiences of love to say that the world of love is here for everyone in each moment. See, listen, and feel the love. Use any disharmonies as indicators that there is another way for love. When you feel an absence of love, what else are you feeling? Anger, impatience, fear? Ask yourself what it is that you are experiencing. Are you willing to be present with that experience until it dissipates and then replace it with gratitude? Utilize gratitude to remember that love is available instead of whatever ails you. Trust love, choose love, and be love. Love shall be home wherever you are when you make it your primary focus.

The Cat and the Mouse: The Question or the Answer?

A little mouse runs to me. He nuzzles under my leg.

"Hello," I say.

"Hello," the little mouse replies. "How happy I am that you have chosen to listen, my friend, for I am a wealth of knowledge. While I shiver in the feeling of fear

in the corner—and yes, if you would like to help me that would be much appreciated—I am scared without anything more to add to what I feel. The cat is clever. I am a lot bigger than this little mouse body. But if I am soon gone from this life I will still be wherever I am. I can't leave. I am always here, which exists as wherever here may be. Some water and food would be nice, Madam. I am here to offer you myself."

Jessie speaks now. "Yes, it's very loving for this mouse to generously offer himself to you, my beloved mother. And it is also with love that I lick my paw. Love. The morning has begun and I am doing some hunting. Prrrr." JJJ gives me a hug. "I love. I love you. I love me. Life feels warm."

In this world of now, where all is what it is, love and peace are here. I serve Rumb some water and walnuts.

"Mouse-Rumb, do you have more to say??"

"It's time for me to go now. You have absorbed my message and I must continue with my own focus."

Does this mean he is leaving the house? Is he staying in hiding? Is he to become JJJ's meal?

"If you would be so kind as to open a door, I may be leaving ... and I may not."

"JJJ, is it okay with you if I do that?"

"Yes, Mother, you know I love the fresh air. I would like to go outside as well."

"You humans have been socialized to expect answers to all questions. Learn to stay in the inquiry, my friend." Suddenly Rumb, JJJ, and I share one voice. Whom are we speaking to? Who is answering?

As I remain in the question a beautiful event occurs. A bird lands directly in front of me, eating in glee. This one is eating something from the ground, dancing in celebration. Suddenly I am transported into the Garden of Eden. As I remain at my computer, I find myself in Heaven, where all beings are in joy and at peace and in oneness. I hear the world singing to me, "We're eating, Laurie, my friend. We're eating!"

I go to take a shower, and there a little violet light appears. It is Rumb. I do not know if he is sending me this light from where he remains on Earth or if he has passed over.

"I'm sending you love," I say to Rumb.

"There is no one to send love or receive love," he retorts. "Love is already programmed into every cell. You need not take that job, for it can't work. Love has no sender and receiver. Love truly is!"

Now I feel Rumb nesting deep in my heart. I am so happy that I can feel love pouring through me and filling up everything. JJJ enters, jumping onto the edge of the bathtub, making a gleeful *mrrrrrrrrr* sound. As I look into his eyes, he flashes me a picture of a book so I make a mental note to write this down later.

Later, when I am dry and dressed I go to my desk to write. JJJ jumps up brushes his face against mine. We continue to exist in love's inquiry.

Waves of the Water

Unconcerned with any of the societal ways, the waves of the water play. Separately moving while still of one overall motion, they splash. They explain that they have chosen prior to incarnation to come as a team. Never alone, they forever watch out for one another. Always in touch with attunement to themselves as one, competition and proving of oneself doesn't enter their unique culture. They seem to be following music that comes from within. Otters acquiesce to their choreography, happily moving in a similar rhythm.

The waves are immersed in a dance and a song that connects them. Music evolves from their movements, meeting the air. Existing in a compelling rhythm, they are taken by something so beautiful that my eyes water. Water beings appear. They are angelic but have human characteristics. They seemed mesmerized by what they hear in the water's motion, but they open their eyes and acknowledge me. They recognize me. I am still warming up to them.

A female child of the water takes me aside to show me a game they play called "swa." You and your partner agree to "swa" each other twenty times in one day if you sign up to play. A "swa" is a way of breaking any pattern that interferes with your brother or sister being fully alive. You note any mental, physical, or emotional patterns that your partner is unconsciously practicing and find a way to kindly jolt that person into a new mode of behaving. You must be quick and make up new swa all day. Swa are done in a playful kindness. For example, you might dance into a partner's contraction so that she or he warmly unwinds.

The water child waves into my jaw, taking my attention, causing me to interrupt a habitual thought and to relax muscles that had been tight for many years. She helps me. This playful way of assisting one another is surely something many people can benefit from. This group is fully committed to helping each other as they serve life, living as vehicles for whatever new information and aliveness come about. Amplifying the sun's warmth and the energies of grace, they are full. Love is what they know. Other games don't interest them, although they seem to have no judgment of anything that anyone else chooses for a life path. They are fully immersed in what they do and very friendly to all who cross their path. We are all familiars to them. People jump into them. They hug these people completely, not missing any part from toe to head, accepting each one exactly as Creation made them!

Bathing with the water children, feeling included as though I am one, I notice that anger in my muscles evaporates.

I feel sun calling me with great strength. I realize that when I follow my inner guidance no matter how odd it seems, I become happy, fulfilled, and blissful.

The Sun Speaks

One day, alone on the porch, I hear the sun speak.

"You are an astro-projection. You are a piece of light and a sound that I sent to the Earth and yet you remain here with me, millions of miles away simultaneously. The personality is a dream. It can be a fun dream if you choose it this way! You forget who you were and become attached to that dream, and from there all problems occur. Now, remember me as primary and all you hunger for is forever satiated. Any problems are simply light and sound in need of harmonic adjustment, and that occurs in an instant, simply by asking."

Trusting the guidance, I notice what the personality is: a light, a sound, a method of loving in duality, a metaphor, a dissolving. I slip back into the unconditional love, peace, and joy, and it is here I remain.

Lil, the Baby Sun, chirps out, "Look, Mom-Dad Sun. If I shine a flashlight into the dark, light appears. If I beam darkness into the light, light appears also."

A funny memory emerges. I remember my parents before I was born. I remember that I chose them in unconditional love, and that it was in unconditional love that they chose me. I notice that each area of pain we create with our ego is a gift, bringing the light to what we need to heal. I remember that my purpose is simply to laugh in a way that inspires others to laugh with great joy. I remember that I am a spirit who receives a personality like a costume. This makes me laugh, at birth, deep inside, as did my new name, Laurie Moore. I remember that I was welcomed and this filled me with glee!

As I remember this, crickets, light beings, and birds begin to sing outside. I live in a dream and so do we all. There is room for everyone's dream to exist at the same time.

"Everyone is invited. Nobody is expected. All religions are at last the same. All stories come down to one sound," Father-Mother Sun proclaims in tune.

I hear Liaya the bay tree singing as eternity outside. A quiet softness fills the room where these fingers type. A thought occurs to me that being a political party is another way of the ego proving its existence, choosing a team. I belong to something much greater, feeling the place inside where I am every political party, ,every religion, the cry and the laugh, the archetypes I admire and the ones I do not like. I am all and all is me, and so what is there to do but forgive? Only love is needed.

"Come home when, if, and how you choose," said Father-Mother Sun, "because, my Loves, you are already home here and now. You always were. My story is an eternal beginning and you are my children."

Animals of Many Species Invite Us Home Via Participation in Life

Many animals are awakened teachers in furry or feathered form. You may find your animal family members and friends nudging you toward peace, joy, playfulness, generosity, and love that is kind and available in any circumstance. As we learn to hear, see, and feel the communications of the animals, we awaken our natural heart-telepathy. We move into states of graced unconditional love. Animals will not let us communicate with intellect that is separate from the heart. To understand an animal's communication, one must fall into resonance with the universal heart!

Unconditional bliss, happiness, and joy beckon you via animal friends. On this planet you will be
encountering instant enlightenment awakenings. Your life can be a daily event of awakenings. It is your choice. The animals are here to help.

While people were thrown and hurt by the December 2004 tsunami in South Asia, many animals went to high ground. A major networking of information occurred among animals, who still listen to the messages of sun, earth, water, and air. They knew where to go.

When we listen to animals, we return to the sun, the moon, and the Source of all life.

Some people will choose to continue to study the way to create troubles. One who utilizes life to study the methods for creating troubles will create incredible depths of misery. One who utilizes life to study and share the light will merge into light. Situations of preferred and non-preferred feelings will move through all like clouds move through a sky. Try an inquiry with light as an experiment.

As we create our intentions and choose where to put our consciousness, the planet will reflect the mass experiences of our individual and collective focuses. Your animal friends encourage you and invite you to participate in love. Trees sing of this reality. If five people look at a vase of flowers from different angles, each will see a different picture. Why is this called subjective instead of objective? If you each take a photograph with the best equipment, you will still have different pictures. Why argue about who is right or wrong? It is all right. It can all happen simultaneously in love's truth, which carries many varied reflections. Each person is here in his or her birthright to have an experience. Many experiences can exist as true ones, simultaneously. Animals accept this, are at peace with this, and live in peace with this. We have enlightened role models all around us. For enlightenment and happiness, consult your dog, bird, bunny, horse, cat, or other beloved animal friend!

If an animal in your life is experiencing a challenge, there is disharmony somewhere in your consciousness. You are not bad or wrong, sweet ones. You are blessed with an opportunity to expand into greater light and wholeness! As you notice your animal's trouble and assist your animal in returning to harmony, know that your animal is doing you a great service. Your animal is assisting you in returning to your full potential, a more harmonious existence.

When an animal is having discomfort with the physical body, the emotional body, or with you, there is something profound for you to learn. Great news: you are being asked to learn LOVE. Let go of perceiving that this animal is "a problem". Instead, look for what is being called forth from you. More laughter? Compassion for another? Kindness toward self? Another benevolent quality? Animals often call out for us to make positive changes in ways that draw our attention. When you learn to listen to your animal friend, who speaks through the heart, soul, and infinite rather than the confines of the intellect, this "concept" shall become something you feel, witness, and experience.

"Come play in the bliss, my friends," the dolphins say.

"Be the joy," says Jessie Justin Joy, my feline teacher.

Animals Live Ecstatically with their Creator
There is an erotic existence simply in living in alive waves. We may feel fulfilled, as though we are the completion shared by lover and beloved. This is a natural
way to feel. Existing in the emotional, mental, and physical realms as a focal point of existing in the soul realm and the one universal heart is the way that
animals experience themselves. As we allow ourselves to surrender to this depth of experience, we find that we are eternity and oneness experiencing a personality in

motion. When you experience this, you may feel like you are orgasmic in every chakra with Universal flow, with all that is. This is complete, ecstatic ONENESS. You are lover and beloved, female and male, as is everyone in a very erotic, wonderful, respectful, life giving-receiving way. You are made of light. Your beingness is orgasmic energy in motion in all chakras. To be alive is to be life in completion with itself.

    No drugs are needed for this gift of life. These natural states of bliss and completeness are designed to occur within you. Such experiences can happen during solo meditation, walking in nature, while making love with your loved one, at work, in the grocery store. You find that there is ONE LOVE, one mind, and one physical fabric alive within the world. There is one to forgive: the mind that forgot the heart. There is no one out there but YOU, Beloved and Lover. The animals know this to be reality.

    The cosmos is in universal love with itself as one. Each person is worthy of remembering this in his or her human-body experience. When they acknowledge what is possible, women turn menstrual cramps into ecstasy in the body. An "unpleasant mood" becomes only a disharmonic chord incapable of interrupting a deeper peace and pleasure. People use instant manifestation to transform pain back into harmonic pleasure. Awareness grows of chakras beyond the seven commonly discussed. We discover that we reflect life in many energy centers while existing as all of life. The personality we most identify with currently is simply our microphone for a lifetime, our place of learning and giving, receiving and transforming so others may evolve after us. We are strands of evolution.

Trust your instincts. There is a level of incredible body and light-body bliss available beyond what you/I/we/they/us have so far encountered. Ask the stars, the dolphins, the whales, and the other animals to assist you on your journey into the new Heaven-Is-Now Realm. Ask that your experience always serve and be given to the Light and Love.

The animals have taught me to remember that I live in a realm in which each person is fully whole—female and male complete within themselves. Everything we think we experience in response to another we actually generate within ourselves. While we think that life circumstances lead us to have feelings and thoughts, might it be the opposite? The giraffes say to me by transferring feeling experiences into my awareness that experiences are the "out-picturing" of the feelings. Thoughts are the bridge into the 3D world, where reflections of our creations show up tangibly.

Feline Guru Jessie Justin Joy says, "Dream your life into existence, my friends.... This is the old way and the only way for unconditional joy!"

Elephants say that they find trunk movement to be ecstatic. Giraffes enjoy Divine ecstasy in their throat. Migrating birds can experience the delight of oneness in the group when the leader (who is following the group heart) glides all through the air. Allow your body to create her/his

own dance of movement by closing your eyes
and following all impulses to discover new realms
beyond the body but felt in the body. There is
nothing to do with the energy of which I speak.
It just is. IT emanates as whole, complete life.
The sun knows this well.

Grasshopper, Bird, and Owl Reassurance
A client toward whom I have extended much love,
care, and kindness calls to tell me that I am
responsible for her being late. I had suggested
to her that she come on time, in order to make
the most of her sessions. She calls to say she
didn't realize that she had been late, but it was my
fault. I feel sad and also this seems funny. I
have heard the same story before. She blame
her parents for many disappointments she has
encountered in her adult life. Her husband is the
source of her dissatisfaction. Her last therapist did her
wrong.
How I wish to help her discover the joy of
responsibility.
How much happier she will become if she might
say, "I apologize to myself and to you for being
late. I'll do my best to be on time." Peace awaits
her.

She is surprised when I tell her that she is responsible for her timing. She expresses that the intensity of emotion she feels in her sessions causes her mind to drift on the way over.

As a result she makes wrong turns and arrives late. Because I am her therapist, this is clearly my fault. As I listen to the convoluted thinking, I notice that a grasshopper is near me. This little grasshopper understands that the ascension into unconditional awakening is available in all circumstances. The amount of resistance we people have at times to simply saying, "I am sorry" is causing massive tension all over the planet. The grasshopper and I feel elated with the gift of being. I begin to take note of any little thoughts I practice in my mind that leave me non-responsible for my experiences.

For this, I apologize to self, to cosmos, to all. As I apologize I feel little threads of relief untying all over my body.

I apologize to the client for anything I may have done to contribute to her coming late to a session.

She says she is distraught and traumatized because I asked her to come on time. A sensitive chord is being touched in us both. I feel sadness arising in us each.

The grasshopper leaps. The powerful force of the waves of self-tormenting between us sends my heart leaping into the air. I find myself high above the land, the structures, and the trees. My heart is set on love.

The choice is available to focus on fears: what I might hit, how I might fall, what if I never re-enter my body, what accidents might occur. Instead my heart is only interested in love. I am in love.

I focus fully on the place inside me that elt so sad to hear the blame. Tension inside this body is shifted into a tighter frustration and then released into joyous love. I release my tie with this woman yet felt tender toward her.

"This is what I prayed for!" I exclaim, because I had wished to fly into space. The waves of existence are becoming larger and larger. Spaciousness grows me into loving joy that holds the unfavorable conversation tenderly as it is dissipating.

Now her voice melts my heart.

While the details of the interaction with this woman were not my choice, I have one desire. I yearn to be in love with all that is, and so I am. And then "I am" is gone. Love loves herself, taking me in.

Safe in flight, yet settled in body, heart waves in a dance. The little grasshopper taking a big jump, the magic of the birds, the beat of my own heart show me how to move. In this heart are waves of gratitude, waves of sorrow, a variety of emotions from both preferred and non-preferred occurrences.

"My intention was to support you in making the most of your sessions," I say. "I am sorry this contributed to you feeling distraught. What is it you want?"

"I can't trust you," she said. "As a professional you should have called me earlier to tell me I was late."

Sometimes the human distortions make me cry.But this time, with the help of my grasshopper friend, I leap instead. I leap out of the delusion. I cackle as I leap. I chuckle at how funny all of us are. I feel embarrassment for us both, embarrassed at the co-creation we are sharing in this miraculous existence.

Feeling how my fear of being judged is magnetizing
absurd situations, I melt into gentleness for the self, for all selves that share one heart. Gentleness grows. Laurie melts again.

Now the humiliation comes firing up in a wave, straight from my organs. As I merge fully with humiliation, strength increases as earth in my tummy, the warmth of my intention, and the power of all I have given this woman, the many times I went far beyond the call. I shrink back into me. Irate at how I am being treated, my shoulders tighten. The grasshopper leaps again.

As I fly into the irate feeling within my being, the sensations change chemistry, waving outward, freely flowing safely. "Take this back. I am trading in this currency!" I exclaim to the universe. Take this woman away and send grateful, responsible souls my way.

Divine Mother is with me to guide and protect me. She makes sure that I am safe at every turn. She appearsas Mary, Gangaji, Ammachi, Quan Yin, a grasshopper, a fawn, a whale, a feline, my friend, this client, me, our hearts, and you.

Divine Ma's many costumes flash before me as my own tenderness in the woman who is angry. I feel her tenderness and mine to be the same.

Eternally safe, existing forever, this dance is protected in the Love of Divine Ma. Participating is the Laurie body, personality, and mind, an artistic expression for one incarnation.

I remember that I am neutral light as my character melts into this. The exquisite opportunity to live blooms through my heart as gleeful overwhelm, again melting all this into a silent reverie.

I say a prayer for this woman. My heart again feels tormented. As I fly into the torment it subsides. I feel equanimity. The waves of life keep going. Inside these waves is a peace that hugs.

The next day she cancels her sessions with me and I feel relieved. Two of my all-time favorite clients call to come in. Two new clients schedule, appear on time, and express tremendous thanks. I thank Divine Mother, grasshopper, birds, and my heart for this gift. The tapestry of us all has created a wonderful change. The new scenario with new characters is attractive. I dive into this attraction again, and Laurie dissipates. Awe loves.

As I land more deeply back into my body, calmness spreads. Later I drive downtown to the grocery store. I see many faces—some happy, some sad, some confident, some desperate. I wish to share bliss with others. Hungry and somewhat cold, we gather in the check-out line. Winter has come and people were not quite ready, not bundled up, still thirsting for a last sip of the summer sun!

Many of us in line are shivering. Some are

gossiping about fears and complaints. Others share gratitude, bliss, and love, and we are full. All in a grocery line. The temple is wherever we are.

Then dullness erases the bliss. Into this I fall. In here is a deep peace, again relaxing Laurie into this.

I notice that one of us has not brushed his hair. One of us has spent hours putting on makeup and hair dye. They look very similar. I see the sweetness in both faces. A light is in the center of each one's heart. Some are in deep love and some in deep despair.

You may find yourself feeling tenderness for people who once annoyed you as you realize that their habits are yours in some other form. You may find yourself taken over by a peace and love that have no limits, no cause, and no reason but their own existence. You may find that everything you once held dear has become secondary to the immense love light pouring through.

Trust, my friends, for the new dawn is being created. Our life here is an art piece. You may find that I am you and you are me.

The animals have patiently guided and waited For the humans to return to love, bliss, and peace. They teach through kindness and compassion. They also teach by reflecting the shadows in us. When we allow, they teach by reflecting our love and magnificence.

If an animal has taken your attention, know that she or he is bringing a Divine message to you.

Recently, as two clients drove off from a workshop, my friend the owl approached. This owl lives by our home. This owl lets me know when I am on track in awakening. This particular couple had chosen unconditional joy. They came to the session blaming one another but left having apologized and thanked one another. The owl appeared to say, "Trust that you too will take on the Divine gift of wings. Choose love. Let conflict be the cause for forgiveness and tenderizing. Melt deeply into what you feel to find a home that is sweeter than any conflict's appeal.

"You are becoming us. We have always been you. You are becoming what was once left behind. You are returning to complete love. You have always been free, and now it is your time to remember who you really are, what once was, and what forever is. Be Love. Be Peace. Be Joy."

Birds sing a variety of tones. The grasshopper comes to visit and leap again. The choices I make echo in how life carries me. The wind bellows in love.

White Gulls

They appear between ocean and land, human and ether. They live as physical beings as well as reflections in dream time. Dispersed into the Earth realm, the energy of lightness, they float, beckoning softly. I experience this calling they offer as Divine Mother, distilling the heart into a very light service-vehicle of purity. It is a fresh new energy they usher in, devotion re-flavored. The energy encourages one to give all personality traits to the light each day, the preferred and non-preferred.

"Here," the gulls express, "each experience is recycled into light. It's a mass cleansing for all Earth beings. Keep giving all of it to the light. You will feel wings lifting your heart and soul. Our wings live in you."

They speak with energy, translated here into words: "You will find humanity's patterns as well as your own. You will dream of white birds, white mythic animals coming to receive and take you to a new understanding of what we are. Go with them. Their journey is delightful and their wisdom is pure."

Recently a big white bird glimmering in the air but without a physical body landed on my pillow and told me, "All your dreams are now true. The veils between the seen dimension and other realms have lifted for many of us at this time."

The dreams this bird was referring to were with me before birth. Some of you out there will recognize it as your own. I incarnated with a dream in my heart that the world would turn itself inside out, back into a heart of love: unconditional universal ONENESS love. I arrived back on Earth in the sixties and was very disappointed at the outcome by the nineties.

Now the dream has come true in my being. Here I find there is room for each preferred and non-preferred emotion and experience. Peace holds this all. This reality of world peace lives in the hearts of all who know it. However, it is not measured by like-minded group realization nor is it dependent upon perceptions of outward relationships. This ONE-LOVE is within each heart, allowing the cleansing of all ego aspects and occurrences. We are light holding ego. Ego can even look good—like someone doing service, like someone in attached love, like someone helping another. All levels of attachment to anything are ego. Filling up another's cracks with yourself is ego. Looking for wholeness by using another's energy is ego. Ego isn't bad, but it is a minute fraction of our highest capacity for fulfillment.

Being side by side, connected in the universal heart and each connected to his/her own light source, allows us to dissipate through ego, right into what is holding ego. There is no need to end ego. The voice of ego has continuous presence in each. By welcoming the thoughts of ego contained in the emotional fabric embedded in the physical fabric, we are taken home in peace via ego's expressions.

As we give it all to the white light, golden light, or violet light, we become light, and the only interest is BEING light. The light becomes us. The Divine Mother has us in her lap and simultaneously she is in ours. However, in this process all our personality traits, talents and strengths, shadows and weaknesses, quests and questions come into full vibrancy. The exquisite love and joy we feel when we experience ourselves as images of ONE LIGHT are incredibly fulfilling.

    I was often afraid to trust this fully so I took time to interact with life rather than to melt into it. Once skeptical, afraid I might lose everything, I resisted. Yet when I came to surrender each moment each day as best I can, the opposite proved true. Each time I allow the winding road within my heart to merge into whatever occurs, spaciousness in love happens. Conflict becomes an opportunity to discover unconditional love through the experience of attached love. I find that everyone in my world is a face of this one LIGHT! Being love takes over seeking or giving love. LOVE IS ALL literally in the body/mind/heart experience of something much vaster and grander! Through any structure or encounter, this can be found.

Animals living in your human homes show up as unique individuals. Simultaneously they are aware of the shared light that emanates them into existence. Be given to this light and your uniqueness is enhanced, never stolen, as role-modeled by many animals. If an animal you live with is ill or emotionally upset, they are inviting you to discover something new within yourself. These friends are altruistically allowing your unresolved ego aspects to move through their body. Heal yourself at the deepest level and assist your animal's health by doing so. Celebrate your animal's willingness to be ONELOVELIGHT!

"I hope this is of help to your understanding. Be Well, Be Light.... You are Light—everything else is a splintered projection. You are the wings of white light and you are the sun," says Jessie Justin Joy on behalf of all animal friends.

"Let your inner knowing be your compass now. Charts, dogmas, and systems are forever available, but you are the truth. Only the wings of the heart can set you into the liberation of fully embodying who you are. Trust your own interpretation beyond anyone else's. You were born into your own dream and you deserve to fly there. Your life is your creation and study. Your life is your art piece and your masterpiece. You know the truth

of your soul more than anyone else. Fly free. Be gentle. Allow the arms of the sun to hold you and the wings of the birds to guide you. You are forever free. You are living in a poem. You are safe."

Deepening My Understanding with Felines

I am learning a great deal from cat companions. They guide me to see that my soul is married to this body for one incarnation. Transformation, learning, and evolution in motion are catalyzed through this union. My body is a temporary housing for my soul. My soul is temporary guardian of my body.

Cats have reorganized my thinking on what a body is. I am learning that I am in a relationship with my body much in the same way that I am in relationship with a human friend, an animal friend, and all of life. When I treat my body with tender love, she trusts me and confides in me. When my body and soul mingle in connected points of gratitude, ecstasy occurs. Cats, who know this bliss well, can be found rolling on the ground, jumping from high places, and darting up trees in delight.

    The human body is a highly devoted being. Each cell has its own tone, purpose, intention, and vibration. Each cell is delighted to serve existence. Many cats stay very attuned to each sensation the body feels. Each cell has strong intention to serve the soul that has chosen to

    The human body is a highly devoted being. Each cell has its own tone, purpose, intention, and vibration. Each cell is delighted to serve existence. Many cats stay very attuned to each sensation the body feels. Each cell has strong intention to serve the soul that has chosen to marry and mingle with the overall body that the cells support. When loved, the body responds in musical tones that soothe and empower the soul, and generate joy.

When I view the world as endless opportunity to harmonize with wellness, I am supported in many directions with transforming a health problem. Health problems come to almost all beings. As we listen to the communications and feel the flavors of physical challenges, we rest in the temple that remains peaceful during turbulence. It's like the eye in the storm. We can simultaneously feel both the eye and the storm, as my cat friends know. We can seep our consciousness into the layers of both non-preferred and preferred physical sensations and emotional flavors that live within our being.

What the mind labels "pain" is the act of resisting. This lesson is learned again and again, sometimes via emotional experience and sometimes via physical. Feline Shera, a shamanic healer, reminds me again that pain is a disharmonious chord. This chord is playing music in the body to get our attention. Try to lovingly welcome the chord and simply be with the chord as is, feeling fully into the vibration. From there, seek out methods to assist the chord with returning to harmony. Cats exist in this way.

Methods to support the body's harmonizing can include any Eastern or Western medical modalities as well as time in nature, doing what gives you joy, and singing to music that is uplifting and balancing. These are some examples, but you can find many ways to assist yourself with returning to harmony.

The body lives in temperature, lights, and sounds. It is weakened by judgments. What we put into the body can be converted into love by simply loving. When we decide that particular creations are good or bad, we feed our body's judgment, and this can cause the body distress that may be experienced as emotional or physical discomfort. It is valuable to treat these discomforts with whatever is needed for physical transformation.

Cats move as the river does, when creations come and go. They befriend what arrives. In this practice they find harmony that holds the favorable and non-favorable experiences that are fleeting.

More Cat Wisdom

Felines purr in devotion to the sun, moon, and Earth. Many are leading humans into the light-body dimensions. There is a way of experiencing life in which a person will identify her/himself to be light itself. Cats know that movement of emotion, thought, action, and sensation is a vehicle for the still sun that is permeating endlessly. The awareness of the neutral light in the middle of all interactions is a love that cats emanate. This strikes a chord so deep in my heart that I am called in love and devotion to my friend, the sun. Cat wisdom brings me to my knees in gratitude. I am overflowing with thanks in my heart to Creator and Creation for making cats.

As I sit with my feline, beloved, Jessie Justin Joy, facing the sun, I return to a place of complete stillness inside myself. From this place, three days of griping and complaining are transformed into light. Diminishing into nothing, these feelings of discontent wash me clean. Only gratitude for this great mystery, this miracle of life, remains.

Deep in the core of my light body, which I find through all my chakras melting into ONE heart, I am forgiveness. I see all beings around me as myself. I can only love. I need no reason to forgive or love. I simply am forgiving and I am love. My choice is to extend this to all who come before me: the dream I have co-created. I feel my cat beloved, tending to me, sending this awareness through me, reminding me that it is my own.

Cats of all shapes and sizes are diligently and devotedly remembering the realities of light and oneness back into existence. As well as being individuals, all the cats are an expression of one vibration that adds a unique peace and jubilance to Earth. For the cats, all life is a dream. In what we call a waking state they are interacting with the flow of energy that moves through life—slow, fast, large, small, little, big, rapid, slow. This is delightful! Cats are in Buddha states in which they both witness and feel every little ripple of life moving through their muscles and blood with great sensitivity.

Cats understand that their physical bodies are costumes they use to play and express their essence. When a cat is in a sleep state she may remain fully
conscious, highly alert to all that is going on around her. A cat senses her entire world inside herself. She/he
he is sensitive to occurrences, people, animals, and plants outside herself, as though they live inside. A cat is in telepathic heart union with beings both physically near and far away.

As humans we may come to understand that we are intricately connected to all lives around us. We may discover that life, which appears to be outside us, is also within us. We may begin to find that what is in our heart is all around us. There is no line between the inside and outside. We can find that all life exists in our heart. This understanding may occur in grace or through a practice of attentiveness to feelings. This understanding will arise if one communicates with animals. Animals do not communicates with animals. Animals do not respond to intellectual discussion separate from the essence of life. Cats converse in connection to the one pulse that beats through all life. By learning to talk with cats, we open doors within our own awareness. Our existence harmonizes. Our senses sharpen in compassion for whatever life presents. We feel life creating itself through us.

As we merge fully into sensation and feeling, emotions come and go; inspired feelings of awe, reverence, devotion, beauty, and love carry us. We may find, as the cats understand, that deeper neutral warmth gives birth to all these feelings.

Humans are invited to discover that we, like cats, are made of light. Our personalities and bodies are costumes we choose for the sake of a particular service to be offered, lessons to be learned, and gifts to be shared. In the final reality all is love. We are loved and loving in all circumstances.

Cats may be fully focused in one physical location while simultaneously lending their soul to another situation far away. In love's reality, there is no distance. A guy named "Anonymous

Big Cat" shows up frequently in the ethereal for my studies, but has not revealed his physical whereabouts. Some animals come to speak to me long before they present themselves to me in the physical realm. Some live too far away to visit in the physical realm. My feline friend Sno lives in San Diego but sends her presence to me in Santa Cruz. Many of my clients report soul visits from feline Jessie, who helps them with their lives.

    A human might misunderstand a cat when a human is stuck in an emotional realm, perceiving the emotion to be ultimate reality rather than a passing flavor. Sometimes humans project their own discomforts onto cats when the cats are handling their challenges with ease. When cats are ready to pass over, they often work to bring their human friends to peace before they go. Cats commonly understand that the passing of their body is only the passing of an outer shell. They move with the layers of change when it is time to go. Their soul will never separate from their beloved human companions.

I have learned that there is no reason not to love and no need for a reason to love. Love is simply a glorious option. It exists and will carry us when we give ourselves to it. In my light body I remember that all people are the lovers and beloveds, children and parents, siblings and colleagues, beyond assigned roles. Only the light is. In this light each being emanates as a simple quality. Some beings are compassion. Some are joy. Some are laughter. All beings are welcome to utilize the library of every single quality that exists! Simultaneously, each being emanates a foundational quality from the time of birth to the time of passing back over. I thank Jessie the cat for bringing me to this awareness, this moment. His love is so pure and devotional that it takes me into surrender to love.

Jessie's experience of self is fluid energy and a bright light permeating outward into all that is. Jessie Justin Joy says, "Trust each person to come to this awareness in his/her own time. Be playful. It's fun."

Thank you, Jessie. Thank you, cat-teachers.

Birds Singing Love

While listening to a choir of birds, my heart sings too. Birds of many sounds, birds of many bodies, birds of many colors all sing at once. The many tones that could create dissonance become a profound harmony of love. I notice that I am love. I find that everyone is only love. The skin and muscles we wear are love.

 Dissolving into this love, I am not an identity. Quiet in which one sound and light live is taking place. Laurie is a set of ephemeral concepts and energies from many memories—my own, society's, and my ancestors'. These scenarios are rising and falling within the Creator loving herself. I dissipate into bird song.

 As I water the garden I re-find identity, experiencing that I am you, you. You are deeply loved. There is nowhere to hide from this big pulsing love as Sun converses with Earth at sundown. In their conversation, Sun and Earth merge as one. Animals, insects, plants, and I are engulfed in love, as colors come and go. I slip back into time and leap forward into time simultaneously. A call forward from a call long ago is creation. The Earth's many creatures are in loving momentum. Although Earth, like us, has hurts and wounds, she remains in love.

Fiercely, gently, quickly, slowly, love beckons. Birds sing the many qualities of love. Deep in the earth, a drum beats, settling the bird chirps in rhythmic faith. Profound eternity is here, and next an emu arrives on our driveway. We do not know from where he came, but he is sitting with Jessie the feline, conversing. Jolted back into the littleness of myself as person and personality, I break into laughter. I look at the very tall bird and furry cat together. Creation is touching, joyous, and funny!

Union with Turkey Vultures

I walk in the desert in Loreto, Mexico. I come upon the body of a turkey vulture whose incarnation has ended only moments ago. Sprawled in total surrender, wings spread, chest to sky, he is transitioning. I sit with my friend as he moves into the ethers. In love, we commune.

I walk on. I find three live turkey vultures. We perch together. They surround me. One circles, waves, and flies only a few feet over my head. One shows me how to take off into the sky. Although my body cannot, my soul flies with my friend as my body receives great cleansing. They take me in as family. Freedom to know myself waves in ripples of sensation through my muscles, as all life enraptures me. Fresh air tingles through my nose, inviting my soul to lean into faith's embrace.

I understand these selfless masters to be the transformers of the physical world. They take what is no longer needed as food, composting it through their own beings. I feel honored by them as I honor them. The difference between life and death, costume and no costume, shows itself to be one uni-verse. One uni-sound with no end or beginning exists in love. All temporary creatures, expressions, and occurrences rise and fall within this one lasting love.

Love dissolves my heart and soul into one essence as thoughts dissolve. I become the lover and beloved in embrace within my own heart. In exquisite orgasmic union, life vibrates as forest, bird, person, breath, and air.

Only love is left. All fabrics of creation are saturated with this love. Living is the Mother's milk. Our lives are Divine Ma's arms. All animals and people are her children. Only love is here. These words do not come close to this of which I speak and am.

I am you, dear friends. You are me. This message is expressed by the turkey vultures in unison as one voice.

A day later I notice a party of turkey vultures gathering in the sky. One by one they join together until twenty-seven have collected. I call to my clients who are with me in Loreto, attending a seminar I am teaching. "These are the friends I mentioned," I say. As Claire walks over to see, one of my turkey vulture friends flies to me. He is right above my head. I wave. He waves back. We share delight. As emotions rise and fall, the turkey vulture friends remain primarily focused on eternity. I feel them living in my heart.

Animals are eager to enter your heart. They will talk to you about the most beautiful life you can live. Be gentle and listen as they call. Give gratitude. Give love. Then you can hear.

Each soul, whether inhabiting an animal, plant, or human body, is of the same consciousness, the same love. Each is a dream of intention, incarnated to express an essential divine quality. Each is surrounded by the sounds, visions, thoughts, and feelings of her dream in living motion. The turkey vulture friends emanate trust, peace, and compassion.

Each person, group, and concept that you find holds a loving intention that is a gift to you.

It is possible to jump to conclusions about others. Often I have heard turkey cultures being condemned for eating trash. Having sat in their noble circle, I find their work to be selfless. When we sit closely with others, feel their hearts, and allow our consciousness to merge with theirs in gratitude, we find their gifts.

Sometimes in the human world we miss another's gift. If we are in judgment about another at any time, we can look into our own heart. We can look at what is stopping us from being at peace and in ease. If we breathe into any feelings that emerge, as turkey vultures do, each feeling dissolves back into love.

We discover that love is involved in every situation. Anything that your mind reports to be other than love waits for you re-harmonize within yourself. Animals are masters of showing people how. Thank you to the turkey vulture family for taking me into vast love.

Whale Teachers

The whales begin to approach me months before I meet them in the physical realm. Their reality is one of continuous devotion. Their experience is of limitless connectedness among all life. They invite me to come into a resonance that reveals the experience of all life to
be one solo light appearing in a variety of shapes, shades, and motions. This awareness allows for a continuing experience that each being is being born and dissolving into this light eternally. Our fleeting nature as individual creatures, within the endlessness of one light carrying us, becomes evident.

Whales approach me long-distance as I sit in meditation outdoors in California. I find myself to become more fluid. It becomes apparent that distance is a type of experience that only occurs in the physical realm. The whales are as close to me as my own heart. They live within me and I within them.

When Ray and I arrive in Molokai, Hawaii, for the first time we are greeted by a dog, Charcoal Beauty, and two cats, Liza and Bef, who live at Molokai Paradise where we stay. These three animal-friends remain our escorts for the duration of the trip. When we open the car doors, the three furry friends, eager to receive us, guide us to the water's edge. I am wondering if the experiences I have been encountering with the whales are my imaginings or truly received expressions from the cetaceans.

On an impulse I call out into the water, "If you are really speaking to me, please show me proof during my time here." Without hesitation a whale jumps into the air. For thirty minutes she splashes her tail up and down.

The whales are alleviating remnants of doubt in the experiences of light that are gathering me up into new ways. They teach me that any thought I think and any feeling I have goes far into the universe, being experienced by others many miles away. In the same way, emotions I experience and concepts I articulate are being felt and articulated by others physically removed from me. Other experiences are moving through my heart, body, and mind in waves. We, all species, are one organism of many faces.

As my relationship with the whale teachers deepens, I listen to what they have to say to humanity. I write this down for my friends.

Stop perceiving human interests as anything other than cultural reflections passing in time. Come to the water to remember that you are home.

Let us handle your love life, your walk on Earth, your work, and all your matters. You have built your life on false constructions and hopes. Let us be the ones who steer you now. Let go of your attachment and dependency on the wilting ideas of societies. Many ideas no longer serve who you are evolving into, what you came to be, and how you yearn to feel life in motion.

Hear the quiet. Melt into the stillness that rocks the motion. Fall into the arms of grace to let us move you gently home through the waters. We marvel at your abilities yet wonder if you can see who you and we really are. You are in a dream. Be in our dreaming in new ways now. Keep letting the water rings expand and open you.

Trust in the dolphins, humble ones. They give soul-food to you: nourishment of glee and joy. Be with that joy a while. Let it integrate. Allow it to permeate in ripples out of you, circling into the arena of humanity. Just be. For today this is your service and your only task. This is all.

People articulate each event, circumstance, and encounter in order to have a meaning. They are putting permanent meaning into all kinds of rituals that only exist as temporary artistic expressions. People are dreaming up concepts of the mind to feel secure, but there is only one vast love, and when you trust in that you are home free.

When your mind attempts to orchestrate situations to be your preferred way, you miss the evolution that aims to take you into blissful territory. When you notice yourself dissolving into love's source you are at peace. Truly all that exists is the One. The ship sailing home is also the water's waves in which this ship sails.

Give up your attachment to any identity that roams around in your consciousness. Your naming of yourself will only clutch you away from the expanding Light that carries all occurrences. You are light. The styles of expression and participation that you choose to embody are simply learning devices. You are neutral light. Be Home as this.

Owl Friend

As I approach the driveway, the resident owl lands in front of the car. With full trust that I will stop my vehicle, she greets me. We face one another in silence that stills my heart with vast, reverent beauty. This majestic being remains standing before me, pulling my heart into hers.

"Do you wish to tell me something?" I inquire. "What you feel is real. Gold light fills the new world. Many can feel this now." Owl Friend reads my thoughts and responds. The words she uses speak to each cell in my body. The quality of faith that these words contain speaks to something in me far deeper than my individual self. I feel the connectedness among all beings.

In a few minutes I will be calling a client, Emma, to answer her question about her canine family member, Buddy. As I approach my house, I am experiencing doubt in my perceptions. I seek affirmation that I will be offering valuable insight. My feeling is that the client's canine companion is full of magical, directed intent, assisting with bringing in new flavors of promise and goodness to our planet.

Buddy is both rejuvenating and leading Emma into deeper trust. My self-doubt comes from wondering if the message I receive from the dog will be understood by the woman. Is the conversation I share with Buddy one that Emma will receive? I also wonder if I am inserting my own way of perceiving into a scenario that may not have the capacity to contain understanding of the energy I am sensing. I am aware that some are trained to think in cookie-cutter perceptions into which the birthing universe can never fit.

Owl Friend fills my heart with golden waves of energy, awe, and confirmation. "Speak to your client. She will understand."

Later, my client Emma confirms that the message I translate for her canine is real to her. She feels the truth of the message: "Golden waves are filling up the world. These waves are benevolent. These waves are in our every cell." The words carry sensations that nourish Emma's heart and soul.

After recently praying to see peoples' intentions as animals do, to not be fooled by appearances or emotional realities that people are able to create as disguises, I become very protected by a light that emanates from the one universal source through this body. I begin to see both the positive and negative intentions in myself and others. I sense our existences together through a combination of compassion and flux that comes from one shared, emanating warmth. Each person and animal is a unique flavor, vibrating from one golden light.

Jessie, my feline companion, via telepathic heart-to-heart conversing, shows me that all life is in motion, evolving in co-creation with our participation. Love, forgiveness, and redirection can change reality right now with our cooperation.

Owl Friend confirms my faith in the unseen help that surrounds us and lives within us. Thanks to Owl Friend, I am able to speak to Emma, my client, with confident care.

Beetle Sibling

During a sacred transition, I hear a knock. Opening the door, I encounter a beetle. I name her Lucy. When she enters our home, she enjoys flying around my head several times. She is a beautiful brown and white striped beetle called a June ten-lined beetle.

Over the next few weeks, Lucy returns each time I am experiencing an inner birth. Whether I am becoming fuller with joy, compassion, or trust, Lucy appears. Each time she visits, she makes her presence known with a knock. She knows just how to move her body against the window to make a sound while keeping her shell well.

One day she decides to stay longer. She sits next to my beloved mate, Ray. Together they listen while I sing a song to them. The next morning I wake up to find Lucy asleep on the bed with Ray, Jessie, and me.

After a shared inter-species meditation, Jessie initiates play. He swats at her. I remind him that she is a delicate little sister. He discontinues the play then sniffs her nose as he would any new friend. He opens his heart to Lucy, who crawls closer to Jessie, brushing against his coat. Lucy snuggles with Jessie, finding refuge under his fur, taking a short nap with him.

When it is time for us to move to a new home, Lucy purposely leaves her shell by our bed and passes on.

A year and a half later when we are settled in our new house, I hear Ray yell, "Lucy is back!"

I run into the kitchen to see Lucy on the counter looking at Ray. She has taken up another body for her current life, a very similar one. He explains that she entered the house, flew a circle around him, and landed in front of him. When she sees me she flies right to me, landing on my leg, where she remains for hours. I put her to sleep by our bed on a little blanket, placing a bottle cap of water nearby.

In the middle of the night I am awakened. Lucy and Jessie are running down the hall together. Jessie is on the carpet. Lucy is up by the ceiling as they stay in pace with one another. Immediately she flies to me and lands at my feet. I pick her up.

Her attentiveness is delightfully soothing to my heart. She assists me in opening my heart and self of many waves into a light that permeates me with unconditional trust in love.

Invitation of the Hawk

Red-Tail Hawk flies toward my car as I drive from Soquel Retreat Haven down the hill. He guides me to weave realities of joy and love with my heart. As I wonder if he is really coming to speak to me, he circles back, landing directly in my line of sight on the telephone wire.

"Sweet Hawk. Sweet Hawk," I say as he looks at me, and again, a faith beyond words takes me in and becomes me.

Come trust yourself, humanity. Listen to the revelations of the animals. These revelations are your own, dancing through your cells, singing in your heart, whispering in the privacy of your own ears, eternally.

Queen Butterfly

On Saturdays, people stop in for an animal communication class.

Before they arrive, Ray notices a royal butterfly on the door. Her body is as big as a beetle. We have never seen anyone like her. Her wing span is over four inches.

She spends the entire day on the door. After the participants leave, Queen Butterfly and I sit together in a natural meditation. Waves of light pull us in. Queen Butterfly emanates wave after wave of clarity without words. She fills my heart. I melt deeper into simplicity than I have previously travelled. I am in awe of her initiations.

Situations I have been addressing in the context of my life appear to be concepts. She takes me into deep essential flavors of life. I realize that the solutions we aim to implement as humans for creating personal to world peace are conceptual. She takes me deeper and deeper into flavor, peace within, wordless.

She sits at the dinner table with us. Her big eyes are very pretty up close. Her wings look painted: gold, white, and black. She and I converse via heart telepathy, energy in motion. We both embody the deep joy that Jessie the feline and I share. We slip into the essence of the heart beckoning care and kindness, appreciation and delights, sorrows and disappointments that Ray and I share. All words leave as Queen Butterfly and I sink deeper in.

I serve her a little water and food. She reaches her arm out but does not partake. She and I remain connected by wonder, confident of our trust in that.

She flies around the house emanating waves of light. Jessie the cat and she run around together. When she lands he kisses her many times, scenting her gently with the side of his face, making her a member of the clan.

She flies into the office with me, so I write an email to some friends about her. Each time I let her outside she flies back in, one time straight to my face. She hangs out on my finger, then my leg, and later my chest. She is beautiful.

These kinds of happenings occur every day, all the time in everyone's lives, but we often forget to notice or experience them. I bet if you sit outside for an hour or so and beam out gratitude, this will become evident!

I am using some descriptions of how we move here and there. I use these descriptions much like a chalice. The honey-nectar in this chalice is the light with which we are beckoned via this incredible mysterious grace. So amazing is the miracle of life that I am shaking with gratitude and sobs as I write. What more is needed? It's all here in amazing grace, moment after moment.

I toss away some troubles I have experienced recently. Those troubles were recycled by generating replicated beliefs of societal assumptions that this and that had happened. Into the compost with glee they went, and a little lonely letting go of the familiar too. My heart aches a bit and then blisses a bit, back and forth. I laugh.

Thank you to this beautiful group of readers for reading these messages. I feel light pouring through me like an inner shower as they are read.

Unconditional Trust in Love

When the time to move from Hidden Valley unexpectedly came about, I was deeply sad to leave my animal and insect friends. I told Jason-Jasona, my spider-friend, who greeted me each day on the stairwell, that we would be moving. The next day she hung herself on her own web. When I called out to her she was happily alive without a body, spinning light. She said she would return.

A couple of years later, I sat meditating in our new, lovely sanctuary home. A tiny little woven blanket, the size of a thumbnail, suddenly fell into my palms. I looked up and saw a spider above me making contact. In my chest I felt a a smile. I felt the presence of my friend. I felt the love that never ends.

Shortly before we moved, my friends the Ravens said, "We will go with you." I thought they meant metaphorically. However, when we arrived in the new home I went for a walk. Two ravens made a U-turn in the sky in order to come back my way and take a look at me. I was perplexed. These were not my friends.

Weeks passed and one day I looked up to see my raven friends from Hidden Valley arrive at our new home. These were ravens that greeted me every day at Hidden Valley. One quacked while the other did three flips over my head to let me know it was them, just as they had done for years. They had received word of our whereabouts from the other ravens after asking

That night an owl looked at me closely and eventually flew over my head into the sky, taking my heart with her into unconditional trust in love.

Animal communication sessions are available.

In person, by phone, and by Skype. All species of animals who are alive or passed over are welcome.

Dr. Laurie Moore

831 477 7007

Laurie@DrLaurieMoore.com

www.animiracles.com

Made in the USA
Monee, IL
13 February 2025

Made in the USA
Monee, IL
13 February 2025